CONQUERING
THE
WILDERNESS

May the blessings
from heaven flow
as you read!
Lana Kristal
12/20/23

CONQUERING THE WILDERNESS

Trusted Tools for Tough Times

LANA KRISTAL

ILLUMIFY
MEDIA.COM

CONQUERING THE WILDERNESS

Published by
Illumify Media Global
www.IllumifyMedia.com
"Let's bring your book to life!"

Paperback ISBN: 978-1-959099-51-2

Typeset by Art Innovations (http://artinnovations.in/)
Cover design by Debbie Lewis

Printed in the United States of America

CONTENTS

ACKNOWLEDGEMENTS

I am humbled by and grateful for every person who gave their time, their editing expertise, and their resources toward the publication of *Conquering the Wilderness: Trusted Tools for Tough Times.* There was a divine plan, and you each played a significant role.

Thank you to my son, Alex Leckie. Alex, the book contains your priceless stories and life lessons, which will help others. Your journey encompassed numerous wilderness seasons, and that's what made you the man you are—you made good choices. You are one of the greatest wilderness conquerors I know. To my beautiful new daughter-in-law, Claire (O'Brien) Leckie, thank you for your counseling expertise and input, and for loving my son. I love you two as big as the sky!

Thank you to my sister, Elizabeth Kristal, and "bonus" mom, Donna Kristal, who are always available to provide a listening ear, honesty, and love. Having family members and friends with whom one can share their heart is a precious gift. You both are a precious gift.

To my extended family members; this book is from my heart to yours. May you receive it with love.

To every friend, counselor, pastor, and healing minister, thank you for sharing your wisdom, compassion, and love. A special thank you to Dr. Douglas and Pam Carr, Barbara Yoder,

Doug and Jodi Firebaugh, Jeff and PJ Smith, Patty Bouchard, Tom and Stephanie Mason, Beckey (Jones) Bingham, Cindy Carswell, Rosemarie Wright, Anita Christopher, Carol Yavruian, Paul Lavelle, Betsy Hemming, Vicki Shea, Sylvia Ioannou, and Steven and Elizabeth Butlin—oh goodness! There are so many others who have spoken words of encouragement into my life; for you I am most grateful.

Thank you to the publishing team at Illumify Media. What seemed a daunting book publication experience turned into a pleasure and a joy. You're the best.

To my earthly father, Frank Kristal, and earthly mother, E. Danelle Kristal, who are in heaven, I would say thank you for providing me a solid spiritual foundation and teaching me how to love.

And to my heavenly Father, thank you God for being gracious. Thank you for your unwavering, unconditional, and never-ending love.

INTRODUCTION

One evening my husband Lance and I were having guests in our home, but he didn't show up. I had no idea where he was. He finally arrived home looking nervous, pale, and pensive. The guests left, we went upstairs, and I readied for bed while Lance, still in his business attire, sat silent on the bench across the room. Hunched over, arms braced on his legs, head hung low, he finally spoke.

"I need to tell you something."

"Okay. What's going on?"

"I was arrested tonight."

Surging adrenaline caused my knees to buckle as I fell onto the bed. I had no precedent for processing what I heard.

"What happened?" I asked with what little logic my brain could muster.

Lance explained. He was in his car, in a parking lot, viewing pornography on a computer and was arrested for indecent exposure. My mind raced. I couldn't catch a breath.

He admitted the pornography addiction started as a teenager. I previously saw minor signs of it, and he promised to get help. I thought it was no longer an issue, but pornography had a vice grip on him.

Lance proceeded to disclose a hidden shame causing him a lifetime trauma. In his early twenties he was sexually assaulted by two men. He didn't share details, and I didn't need to know. Sobs pulsated from the depths of his soul as years of unresolved pain poured out. My husband of seven years lived with this humiliation much of his life; my heart ached for him.

"I am so sorry."

As we got ready for bed there was little conversation.

"I need some time to think," I told him as I slipped into our bed.

"Okay. I understand," he calmly responded.

What does a wife do? Throughout the night I prayed and processed that question as tears soaked my pillow. The place I turned was the source of all truth, which says a wife is to respect her husband. A counselor once told me respect isn't all or none. You can respect some parts of a person's behavior, but that doesn't mean you must respect all of their behaviors.

"What does respect look like in this gut-wrenching situation?" I wondered.

I made the choice to come alongside my husband with compassion. I respected his honesty, his genuine remorse, and his willingness to get help.

The morning sunlight brightening the somber atmosphere of our home was most welcome. I took Lance's hands, looked into his eyes, and as we both wept I asked, "What do we need to do?"

During the following weeks, although neck-deep in a quagmire, we waded through this mess of a wilderness. Thankfully, there were several precious moments.

Lance was on the phone with an attorney and responded, "She's totally supportive." He was quiet while the attorney spoke and then Lance said, "I know. I'm very blessed."

Here was my husband of seven years. Addicted. Ashamed. Devastated. With strength from the Divine, I chose grace toward my husband. I receive grace 24/7/365, so who was I to withhold it from my husband?

Healing rooms are centers where a team of godly people impart compassion and love for those seeking emotional and spiritual support. Lance and I attended one after which he was peaceful although very quiet.

A few days later he walked out on our deck overlooking the serene, wooded ravine and said, "I can hear the birds." I was stunned realizing how deeply the emotional and spiritual turmoil had dulled his senses, but at the same time I was grateful to be watching him slowly be released from the grip of pain, shame, and trauma.

As we jumped over legal and emotional hurdles, he reached out to a church hosting a meeting for those struggling with pornography. He appeared excited to attend and also made appointments for counseling. Healing was happening—or so I thought.

Lance told my son, Alex, he wanted to talk. The three of us sat on our back patio as Lance apologized for the way he treated me and said, "Your mom is the most wonderful wife and mother." He told Alex what a wonderful stepson he was. Suddenly Lance began to sob, his whole body shaking.

Alex looked at me and mouthed, "What now?"

With my arms I motioned a hug. My six-foot two son leaned over and placed his arms around his repentant and remorseful stepfather; it was a picture of grace.

Wandering in the wilderness—we've all been there. Tough times can blow us into swirling fear, anxiety, stress, disappointment, and even depression or discouragement. Hopes and dreams haven't come true or perhaps a painful past hangs around. Problems seem overwhelming and our thoughts surge all over the place. We feel crummy. We just want to feel better.

I have landed in the wilderness after illnesses, surgery, an abusive relationship, job loss, and people I dearly loved dying. When the first tough times came, I wasn't sure how I got there or what to do. In my personal world where things should make sense, they didn't. All at the same time things were good and bad. Happy and sad. Up and down. I hurt due to circumstances outside my control, and also at times because of my own choices and decisions.

Peace and contentment seemed elusive as I asked, "Why? Will things ever change? Will my heart ever heal? Will I ever feel good again? Will I feel joy again?"

The answer? Yes!

Somewhere deep within me I knew with the right tools I could conquer the tough times and navigate them with better understanding, insight, strength, and wisdom.

As we journey through these pages you will learn:

~ How the way you think can change and affect your emotions (Chapter 2).

~ How to communicate effectively and improve your relationships (Chapter 3).

~ How environmental factors influence behaviors (Chapter 3).

~ How to clarify perceptions and realities (Chapter 2).

~ How you can connect with the divine purpose for your life (Chapter 8).

~ How you can have hope on this side of eternity (Chapter 9).

I made it through, and you will too. *Trusted Tools* are here!

Using the *Trusted Tools* throughout the book will help guide you through the toughest times in life and equip you to conquer emotional, physical, mental, and spiritual battles.

Each chapter ends with a *Toolbox*. The questions and reflections give you real-life application to the lessons, ideas, and suggestions in that chapter.

Let the conquering begin!

CHAPTER 1

THE WILDERNESS

On an early summer Sunday, parents, stepparents, and grandparents gathered in our home for a luncheon in honor of Alex's high school graduation. The house, decorated with palm trees, floral garlands, and ocean vistas, reflected his college destination—Hawaii. We dined on luau chicken, macadamia shrimp, and aloha sweet potato salad. Our hearts were full watching videos of Alex's priceless childhood years flashing across the television as graduation gifts were opened and joyful stories shared.

My husband Lance, Alex's stepfather, was fully engaged and helpful as always, although I noticed he was a bit antsy. At the afternoon graduation ceremony, he excused himself several times; I thought he had too much coffee.

That evening Alex, Lance, and I had reservations at our favorite restaurant, but Lance told us to go without him. The emotional exhaustion from the arrest, the legal maneuvering, and revelation of the pornography addiction had been beyond stressful. I figured he was simply tired, so Alex and I went off to dinner. Afterward I helped with the all-night senior party. When

I arrived home Lance was sound asleep, and all was well—or so I thought.

In the morning I had a meeting at my office and as I pulled out of the driveway Lance stood in the garage waving good-bye—in his briefs. It seemed unusual for him to wave good-bye while not dressed, but I went on to work.

Driving home after the meeting I was excited. For the first time in years, I felt hopeful knowing our marriage was coming out of the wilderness. Lance's arrest and revelation of the pornography addiction led us to professional help, counsel, and more prayer than ever. In addition, the support of dear family and friends was beyond amazing. Our marriage was going to be better. We were going to be better, and I felt great!

Lance was gone when I arrived home, and as I chatted on the phone with a friend I went into his office. Sitting at his desk I glanced at his computer screen.

"Stop talking!" I yelled into the phone.

Is this what I think it is? What was I reading? It can't be! I read to my friend what seemed like a suicide note.

Fear. Bewilderment. Confusion. My head raged with explosive thoughts and emotions.

"You need to call your father," my friend said.

I immediately hung up and did so. When my father picked up the phone I read the note to him, and he agreed I needed to call the police. I called several friends who came immediately and within two hours a detective and the police chief were at our home. I invited them in, and they asked me to sit down.

"I can't sit down," I said. "I'm all right. Just tell me. Just tell me. He's dead, isn't he?"

They confirmed the worst. The caretaker at a cemetery found his body. After waving good-bye to me, Lance put on his military BDU (Battle Dress Uniform), got in his car, and drove to a cemetery. Under a tall tree he placed photos of Alex and me, his backpack, and his will. He took out his handgun and put a single bullet in his head.

A dark wilderness engulfed me, my son, our families, and our friends.

Because he was a financial planner and a respected Army Reservist, the media called for interviews, and the story became headline news. They all asked me, "Why?" I certainly didn't have an answer. All I came up with was, "Apparently his desire to be at peace was greater than the thought of enduring more pain."

He never showed me his VA reports and when reading them for the first time a few answers surfaced. He suffered from post-traumatic stress disorder (PTSD), which he never discussed with me. Given he was deceased, and confidentiality was no longer necessary, the team from the healing room shared the rest of the story, which Lance had shared with them. As a young child Lance was sexually molested by a family member.

Although secrets, shame and guilt undermined his life, Lance maintained an outstanding military and business career. When someone takes their own life, the why question is ever present, and there is never a single or adequate answer. With Lance, I sensed he wanted to spare his family, friends, and colleagues the potential humiliation should the the arrest become public. Suicide is never an answer. There are other solutions, which is one of the reasons I wrote this book.

I share this and other intimate stories of my life to save lives, both physical and spiritual. It is my desire to help others understand how to save our physical bodies from harm, and to understand what happens to our body and spirit when we are no longer on earth.

Upon asking Lance's sister's permission to share her brother's entire story she said it well: "If it will save one life it's worth it."

Your life is valuable. Your life is important. And when you get through the tough times, you are a survivor, an overcomer, and a conqueror!

Believe me—after the trauma of going through a divorce from my first husband and my second spouse committing suicide, I knew my body, mind, will, emotions, and spirit needed a lot of help and healing. Through the following months and years, I learned, and am still experiencing, how during even the toughest times we have opportunities to better understand ourselves, and most importantly, heal and have hope.

What are Wilderness Seasons?

Many days I landed in the wilderness. Waking up in the morning my first thoughts were, "What am I going to do about a job?" "How am I going to pay the bills?" "Will my BFF (best friend for life) ever speak to me again?" "Why are they believing that lie about me? It isn't true!" "Will I ever get over this sickness?" "Will I ever get over the pain of losing my baby?"

Life is challenging and uncertain at times. We experience disappointment, stress, pain, and confusion. One thing is for sure, after our world has been rocked by what's happening now, or happened in the past, we wander through our emotional landscape as best we can.

Maybe you're saying, "Been there, done that!" Yeah, me too.

We All Have Them

Wilderness seasons come and go; they may last a moment, a day, or maybe months. Just as if we were wandering in an unfamiliar wooded forest, guides and tools help us get through. The same is true in life.

As you go through tough times, using this guide as a Trusted Tool will help you navigate through them with greater intentionality, direction, understanding, and peace. Be encouraged. You can have hope. You can have faith. You will be peaceful and joyful again, or maybe even for the first time!

What Is the Wilderness?

How and why do we get into these wilderness times? Let's call them tangibles and intangibles. Tangibles are physical, what we see and touch. Intangibles are emotional, mental, and spiritual responses to those tangibles.

Tangibles

~ People—old, new, and current relationships

~ Material possessions

~ Jobs and careers

~ Our physical bodies, our health

These are concrete, the things we can see and touch.

Intangibles

~ Loss of dreams

~ Loss of desires

~ Loss of vision

~ Loss of hope

~ Trauma

~ Change in life circumstances

~ Sadness, anger, and grief related to all of these

A change in a tangible, physical reality results in an intangible response in our soul and spirit. We cannot physically touch these intangibles, but we do respond to them with thoughts, emotions, words, and behaviors.

These tangibles and intangibles will be explored in depth. For now, be aware there is a whole bunch that happens in life to land us in a wilderness season. But it's okay. And while it may feel unsettling to read about chaotic times, keep going and you'll be better equipped to handle life's tough times.

My husband's tangible suicide catapulted me into an intangible and yet very real emotional and spiritual response. What was I to do with the intense pain? How was I supposed to get a grip on the confusing spinning thoughts? Why was I feeling so many conflicting emotions? Why was I reacting all over the place?

What if in the midst of darkness, I saw a flicker of light?

Wonderful Wilderness

What if we learned to make sense of these wilderness seasons? What if those wilderness times could be flipped into something good, something useful? What if during those tough times I could have gone through them with less drama-trauma and more self-awareness, purpose, and peace? What if I had been better equipped to deal with it all? I wasn't then, but I am now.

A tough time can be a good time (for real)!

Eventually I found ways to navigate the wilderness, to gain insight and understanding about myself while going through it, and to be able to move toward my identity, purpose, and destiny. I won't keep these to myself! I will share them right here.

The wilderness can be a time:

~   Where you learn to think differently.

~ Where you can let yourself feel your emotions without fear.

~ Where you can hope again—no matter what.

~ Where you learn what really satisfies.

Really? Yep. I know it's possible because I've experienced it. To navigate these seasons, I turned to support: family, friends, healing counselors, spiritual guides, and prayer. I discovered basic tools to redirect my thinking, which helped calm my emotions. When I became aware of why I thought the way I did, why I felt the way I did, and why I responded the way I did, I got through difficulties so much easier.

Wilderness seasons are opportunities to:

~ Understand what makes you tick.

~ Learn to avoid communication confusion.

~ Go from an emotional wreck to an emotional rock.

~ Put patience to practice (it's easier than you think).

~ Contend for faith and see it grow into hope.

~ Receive love as never before.

And just so you know, to this very day as I go through challenges, I say to myself, "I need to use the tools in my own book!"

TOOLBOX

- ☐ List the tangibles and intangibles which landed you in a wilderness of anxiety, stress, disappointment, or pain. Maybe you're in one right now. Make a note of a past or current wilderness.

- ☐ List next to the tangibles and intangibles what led you there. Soon you'll be better equipped to get through it.

- ☐ Reflecting on these tough times, did you realize you learned something insightful about yourself or others? What brought you to this realization?

- ☐ Are you open to the idea that tough times can turn into times of learning and growing? Why or why not?

- ☐ What do you think would help you get through the wilderness easier? Keep reading and you'll discover more. ☺

CHAPTER 2

PERCEPTIONS AFFECT THE EXPERIENCE

Perceptions and Reality

Everything—that's a strong word and it's true. Every thought, action, and emotion in our lives is filtered through our perceptions. Perceptions are how we view, think about, and discern what we believe to be our reality, what we see and hear. Our perception of the world affects our thoughts, feelings, emotions, words, conversations, and well, our whole life!

After telling me my home was beautifully decorated for the holidays, a friend said, "You should have people over." Her perception was that I had not recently entertained. In reality I had just had two dinner parties. Her assumption was based on her perception, which was not reality.

The way we perceive a situation may or may not be reality. In this scenario a better communication would be to ask, "Have you had people over?" "Have you thought about having people over?"

Fact-check perceptions and opinions with truth and reality, and then determine what's true. Asking questions of yourself or of others helps to refine our perceptions, our thinking, and therefore our opinions. Ask questions. Clarify. Fact check. As mama said, "Think before you speak."

When we tell others what they should and shouldn't do, we project our perceptions, thoughts, values, and ideas onto them. Though our intentions may be honorable and helpful, it doesn't feel good to be told what to do—especially when you're over the age of eighteen.

Reality > Thought > Perception > Feeling > Response

~ Check the facts, the reality of the circumstance by discussing them with another person and using active and reflective listening (Chapter 3).

~ Recognize how and what you are thinking about a situation.

~ Are your thoughts and perceptions accurate?

~ Do your feelings align with the reality of the situation?

~ How and why are you responding the way you are?

~ If you feel stressed, is it based on the reality of the situation? Is your perception of the situation accurate? Can your thinking be adjusted to alleviate stress? (More on stress later.)

As I increased awareness of my thoughts, perceptions, feelings, and responses, I got a greater grip on my emotions.

Using this powerful *Trusted Tool* during wilderness seasons enabled me to conquer destructive, negative thinking and emotions.

Choosing How I Perceive

How we perceive life's situations is a choice. This choice is made with the thoughts in our head which affects our attitude, how we go about our day-to-day living, and ultimately how we experience life. Whether we get through challenging times and wilderness seasons with ease or with difficulty is proportional to our perceptions of ourselves, others, and our situations. See Chapter 3 for greater detail on communication and perceptions.

Victim vs Victor

After major surgery, the huge stress on my body at times turned me into an emotional wreck. During recovery, while spending hours and days in bed, I felt left out and lonely, knowing my friends and family were out having a good time. It was hard, but what could I do? For sure I was bored and at times irritable. Actually, the family caregivers might have used a few other choice words to describe me!

The physical aggravation and the meds were messing with my brain and feelings. I had lots of emotions, and many of them weren't good. Eventually I managed to recognize and call out those emotions, and work *with* them instead of against them. When I acknowledged how I was feeling (lonely, cranky, and physically ill), I had the freedom to change my thinking and perceptions.

A victim attitude says, "Poor me. I'm stuck here. I'll never get better." A victor's attitude says, "This happened and I'm making it through. I *will* get better. I *will* be healed." I changed my perception and made a choice, an action of my will. Was I going to be a mental victim to the circumstances, or was I going to be a victor by making changes in my thought process?

I changed my thinking to conquer a victim attitude by:

~ Reaching out to friends and family for emotional support.
~ Reading only uplifting books and stories.
~ Watching feel-good videos and movies.
~ Accessing my spirit through prayer.

Fight It or Embrace It

When we allow our attitude to shape us and not consume us, the wilderness can be useful. How do we allow shaping?

I've been to Israel, Turkey and Greece so I like to use Bible stories as examples. After experiencing these lands, Bible stories come to life and are tangible. Use your visual imagery and come along.

Did you ever see, or hear about, the movie *The Ten Commandments?* Nearly every year it's broadcast on television. In the story, the Hebrew people (Israelites) were slaves in Egypt for four hundred years. When finally freed from bondage, they traveled to the Promised Land (modern day Israel), which should have taken two to four weeks. They ended up discouraged and doubting, fearful and anxious as they wandered in a literal wilderness desert for forty years! *Wilderness* in this context means "to speak," "to order," or "to arrange" words. The wilderness was an arranging, so what was being arranged? The wilderness can be a place of perfectly arranged order, harmony, and balance. The Israelites forty-year wilderness was an opportunity for them to learn balance, order, and harmony.

What did they learn? The experience shaped their faith, their identity, and increased their understanding of their relationship with God.

Balance, order, and harmony are available to us during the wilderness!

Someone said, "When you're in the desert, don't fight it. Embrace it. You may be there for a reason." This really annoyed me. I didn't want to hear there was some out-there purpose for having to suddenly live on a pittance after years being able to make calculated investments and give away money to help others. I didn't want to hear there was a reason to be single again for many years when my wish was to marry again. I didn't want to hear there was a reason I had to keep waiting for the fullness of my purpose, my destiny, and the fulfillment of my heart's desires.

I didn't want the wilderness, but I was there. And I had a choice: to feel sorry for myself and look at the negatives and fight it or to embrace it, get through it, learn from it, and seek to conquer it. After seasons of aimless wandering through the wilderness, I gradually learned how to embrace it and work with it rather than fight against it. You will too.

No pain, no gain! Once referring to physical exercise, today we apply it to studying in school, relationships, and work or advancing a career. Is it really necessary to experience pain to achieve success and progress? Sometimes. Times of pain and pressure may be useful in moving us toward a desired outcome. Really? Yes! And here is a *Trusted Tool.*

"Even in times of trouble we have a joyful confidence knowing that our pressures will:

1. Develop in us patient endurance.
2. Patient endurance will refine our character,
3. Proven character leads us back to hope.
4. This hope is not a disappointing fantasy,
5. Because we can now experience the endless love of God..." (from Romans 5:3–5 TPT)

What we focus on determines how we get through the wilderness. We'll unpack this in subsequent chapters. For now, realize when we are going through a tough time it's good to ask questions like What can I learn here? How can I get through this with some sort of sanity? Is there a lesson to be learned beyond the situation or circumstance I see in front of me? Is this some sort of character refining I'm going through?

Look for the Blessings

Blessings are divine favor and grace. How can there be blessings during really bad times? When the wildest wilderness times hit and I didn't know where to turn, I turned to the Divine, that is, God. I asked Him to do things. I asked Him for things. And then I had to learn the difference between thinking He was *able* do something and *trusting* Him to do it. After all, He's not a magician we turn to for stuff. Trust is an action. It is believing in God's abilities and believing His best intentions for us. This is implemented through faith. Here is faith and trust in action.

Several large bills were due immediately. My sister suggested I cash in the silver in my safe. I went to the safe, twirled the dial, opened it up, and opened the metal boxes containing the silver. Empty. We suddenly realized I previously had already sold it all. I sat there on the floor stunned. Fear and frustration slammed over me as I thought, "Now what?"

Seriously, here is what I did. I looked up, raised my hand in the air and exclaimed out loud, "Lord, you are my Father, and I am your daughter. A father takes care of his daughter. There has got to be something in that safe I can sell. You promised to supply all my needs according to Your riches in glory in Christ Jesus." I sat and wept. But then! As I began returning items into the safe, old camcorder tapes fell down. (Some of you reading this don't even know what those are. Someone older can fill you in!) I reached inside the safe to straighten them up and all the way in the back, tight against the wall, was a piece of paper. It was the receipt for an investment coin I had purchased.

I called the number on the receipt, and a kind woman answered. I told her about the coin and that I was told by a professional it was worth much less than what I paid. She immediately said, "If you feel you were ripped off, it can be taken care of in extenuating circumstances."

Bingo! She said, "Ripped off." I was surprised with her choice of words and realized the company that sold the coin must be aware of the discrepancy. I asked her what kind of extenuating circumstances qualify. I was reflective listening, repeating what I heard (thank you, marriage counselor). She said to call a coin grading company and inquire about the current value. The company confirmed that the coin was worth only a few hundred dollars. I called the first woman back, and during our conversation I told her I was a military widow. When I said the word *widow,* I was suddenly overcome. Not because of *being* a widow, but because all at once relief, fear, and hope burst to the surface. I couldn't speak. She asked if I was still there. "Yes, I just need a minute," I said. Then I told her I had purchased the coin as an investment the year after my husband took his own life. "His name was Lance," I said, "and if you search his name, you can read all about it on the Internet."

She exclaimed, "My son's name is Lance!"

I chose my next words carefully. "I do feel I was taken advantage of, and I would like a full refund for the amount of purchase. And, of course, I will return the coin." I spoke what I wanted to see.

She politely explained the group in charge of making these decisions met only once a month. I told her I had an urgent financial situation, and if she and they could move this along quickly I would really appreciate it. Two weeks later I received thousands of dollars as full reimbursement for the coin. The blessing? All my needs were supplied. Seek God, and you'll find Him.

 Belief > Faith >Trust >Action

Peaceful—No Matter What

How in the world can we be peaceful when all heck is breaking out in our personal world? It's not easy. Emotions are real and not to be denied, at the same time once we fact-check them with reality, monitor our thinking, and delve into the spiritual we have the opportunity to enter a new place of peace.

I've been able to experience peace during tumultuous times by bringing everything I'm thinking, feeling, and worried about to the divine being called Holy Spirit. This is one of our most *Trusted Tools*. In Chapter 6 you'll learn more about Holy Spirit, for now know that another name for Him is Comforter. You can take all pain, anger, betrayal, frustration, hurt—all of it—to this divine being to help you through it. This was imperative for me in conquering the wilderness. How did I do it? I connected my spirit to Holy Spirit through prayer and meditation. When I just couldn't handle it, in tears I cried out, "I can't deal with all this. Help me!" When my focus on and connection to Holy Spirit increased—seriously! Peace settled in my emotions and spirit.

Growing up, in order to maintain a sense of peace in my life, I've always viewed myself in the middle. In school I often thought, "There are those who get better grades than me, and there are those who get worse grades." Today my perspective is the same. We are more content when we don't compare ourselves to others.

Joy is a spiritual place of well-being and inner contentment. It is a spiritual state, not quite like happiness. Happiness is more transient and dependent on external circumstances. It is emotional. When life is upside down, how do we get to that place of inner joy? The experience of joy may vary from person to person, and I describe mine in Chapter 6.

Purpose in Pain?

What if during the dark times we had guides and tools to help us through and lead us back to the lighter times? And what if during that journey we were molded into a better form of ourselves? There may be a purpose for what you're going through right now or have gone through in the past.

When our dreams are shattered, when the pain is searing, when our finances are in shambles, when our relationships don't work out, when we are struggling at school, when we are struggling at work or home, sometimes it's God; sometimes it's not, and often it's hard to tell the difference. But when we are open to hearing from God, those times are useful. Yes, there can be purpose during the pain. During wilderness waiting:

~ Our hurts can be healed.

~ Our faith can grow.

~ Our hope can increase.

~ Our spirits can increasingly connect to the Divine.

Painful times can be purposeful times.

Patiently waiting opens us—our soul, spirit, and heart—to the possibility of a greater plan. Let's be real, waiting isn't easy and requires patience. Though the outcome of my waiting period was not what I thought or wanted, I eventually learned to trust God more than my own steps. How's that? Read on.

Patience. Now there's a word that rubs against us, but let's look more closely. Patience is both mental and emotional. The Merriam-Webster dictionary says patience is "bearing pains or trials calmly or without complaint." Doing something calmly is intentional, a decision in our thought process. We can choose to be patient by simply realizing we may not have any other choice in a circumstance. By refocusing our thoughts, we can say to ourselves, "I can't change this situation. There's nothing I can do about it right now, so I'll accept it as is." Discernment helps us to know when we can change our circumstances and when we can't. See Chapter 5 for more on discernment.

When we are impatient, we feel restless, anxious and short tempered. We can refocus our impatience by realizing there may be a plan, which we may not currently see.

"But if we hope for what we do not yet have, we wait for it patiently" (Romans 8:25 NIV).

If you're a parent or have even owned a pet, you're familiar with those times when love requires discipline. Discipline comes from the word *disciple*, meaning "to teach." Ideally parent-child discipline stems from love and a caring heart. Love for a child or a pet requires discipline for them to learn lessons.

Just as a parent teaches a child, Father God also teaches us. Wilderness seasons offer opportunities to understand what He wants to teach us, and to see and experience expressions of His love. These seasons are valuable times of learning.

We are not static. We change and grow, and our free-will choices influence the dynamics and direction of that change. During my wilderness seasons, eventually I learned how to:

~ Implement faith.
~ Get a grip on my emotions.
~ Work on not judging others.
~ Be more patient.
~ As "way out there" as it seemed at times, look for God in action.

Redefine Wilderness Seasons

After going through many wilderness seasons, eventually I learned how to clear the foggy lens to see more clearly and then the wilderness took on a new vibe.

A wilderness season can be:

~ A time when you learn what really satisfies.

~ A time when you learn to think differently.

~ A time when you can feel your emotions without fear.

~ A time when you can learn to hope again.

~ A time when you can reach out for help instead of going it alone.

By Design or by Choice?

You Have a Purpose

Were you randomly put on planet earth for no particular reason? No! You are divinely created with a purpose. It's a beautifully inspired journey lasting our entire earthly lifetime. How do we know our purpose? Our purpose is revealed when we seek it out. How? Jump to Chapter 8 for details.

How do we know if our challenging times are (1) a divine plan, (2) due to our own choices, (3) because of the consequences of our own decisions, (4) due to the action of others, or (5) because of circumstances beyond our control like an accident or illness? Sometimes we know and sometimes we don't. One thing is for sure, the Divine Creator genuinely wants what is best for us. Yeah, I agree, it sure doesn't feel like it when all heck is breaking loose. More on that soon.

Whether due to a divine plan, our own choices, or unavoidable circumstances, the *Trusted Tools* for getting through are similar. Here's the deal. Whatever the reason, there are many opportunities to discover and learn more about ourselves during any given wilderness experience. More *Trusted Tools* are coming!

You Are Divinely Created with a Divine Plan

Wilderness seasons happen for a lot of reasons and though we may not understand why, using *Trusted Tools* helps us navigate through them with peace, insight, and understanding. And then—we conquer the wilderness!

The wilderness is an opportunity to develop:

Character	Patience
Humility	Wisdom
Knowledge	Strength
Compassion	Contentment

Other Reasons for the Wilderness

We are being protected from people and events.

We need to better understand our divine design.

Our Divine Creator wants to communicate with us.

Our Divine Creator wants to start something new in us.

By looking for them, opportunities are available for personal change and growth. Good things!

TOOLBOX

◻   Think of a time when your perception of a
     situation wasn't really accurate—let's call it
     like it is: it was wrong. It's okay. We've all
     done it. What made you realize you had a
     misperception? What unwanted attitudes or
     feelings did the misperception create? It's alright.
     Now you have an awareness tool for the future.

◻   Consider life at this moment: your work,
     school, relationships, and hobbies. Make two
     lists: (1) things that make you feel discontent
     or impatient and tell why, and (2) things
     for which you are thankful and grateful.
     Gratitude could be as simple as being able
     to get out of bed this morning. And if you
     couldn't then maybe gratitude is having
     someone or something to help you.

◻   What people, situations, or circumstances
     landed you into an emotional wilderness? What
     thoughts do you have about it? What makes
     you content? What makes you discontent?

◻   Why do you think you were created?
     Considering your passions, desires, abilities,
     hopes, and dreams, what do you think is the
     purpose for your existence?

CHAPTER 3

HE SAID, SHE SAID, I SAID

Ready for a great news flash? You can get through the toughest times in life with less anxiety, stress, and fear. The key is somewhat simple, yet at times we make it complex. Awareness of and improving our communication has a positive effect on every aspect of life.

All day long we're doing it. Thinking. Talking. Listening. Also texting, emailing, tweeting. We use Facebook, FaceTime, Zoom, Instagram, Rumble, and Slack. We talk to ourselves, and we listen to ourselves. We talk to others, and we listen to others. Every day, all day, we communicate. Communication is a key tool.

Our thoughts and words create
a positive or negative atmosphere.
That's a lot of power coming
from our mouths!

A communication wilderness is somewhat common. How and why? Miscommunication leads to misunderstanding, which leads to communication confusion, which leads to raucous relationships. An innocuous conversation could become an argument when we feel we're not being heard (they're not listening to me), we're not being understood (they don't understand what I'm trying to say), or someone says we think and feel something we don't.

When we perceive we're being verbally attacked, our feelings get hurt. We shout accusations and lash back, or maybe we withdraw. This lands us smack dab in the wilderness. How do we avoid it? After all, if we effectively communicated, there would be no more arguments, no more unkind words, fewer broken relationships and hearts, and clearer understanding. Ha! How is that possible? With *Trusted Tools* of course. ☺

Skillful communication prevents misunderstandings and hurt feelings, enhances intimacy in relationships, and can bring peace and clarity to many situations. What does "skillful" communication look like?

What I Say to Me

Do you talk to yourself? It's okay! A powerful tool in avoiding a communication wilderness is an awareness of what we say to ourselves with the thoughts in our head. Have you ever listened to what you say to you? Say what? How do I listen to me? Through your thoughts; it's what you're thinking *about* you *to* you. The dialogue we have with ourselves, whether internal or out loud, is called self-talk.

Self-Talk Awareness

It's insightful when you pay attention to what you say to you. Self-talk impacts our mindset, emotions, behavior, and words.

Positive self-talk helps boost confidence, enhances motivation, and promotes an optimistic outlook. It is a tool for self-encouragement, self-motivation, and self-reassurance, especially in challenging situations.

Negative self-talk, having critical or pessimistic thinking, could lead one to the intangible wilderness of lower self-esteem and self-doubt. Negative thoughts increase stress and anxiety and create a faulty perception of self, situations, and circumstances.

Encourage one another and build one another up, starting with you!

Your Possibilities

Encouraging yourself doesn't mean being prideful or arrogant. It does mean treating yourself with patience, kindness, and love. It means speaking uplifting, positive words to yourself. It means avoiding negative words which tear you down. Jump to the end of the book for affirmations to encourage your perspective of yourself.

 ## Speak nicely to you!

A close friend who is a very kind person said, "I feel like I'm a bad person." My knee-jerk response was, "That is a lie. Who said you are a bad person?" She explained her boyfriend felt that way about himself and told her she was a bad person too. She let his negative attitude become her truth when in fact it was not. An example of a good time for one of those reality checks.

How Am I Lookin'?

When you look in the mirror, what do you see and what do you say? I'm too thin, too fat, too much hair, not enough hair, lookin' scruffy, lookin' good? Imagine looking in the mirror and saying, "I feel good today" or "Lookin' good today" not out of vanity but in a way that is encouraging to yourself.

 ## Your words about you impact your attitude about you!

Try This

Set your phone to ping several times a day. When it pings say something affirming to yourself. Need ideas? Suggestions are in the back of the book.

Notice the differences between positive and negative self-talk in:

Your emotions,

Your body,

Your thoughts and feelings toward others, and

Your thoughts and feelings toward your circumstances.

Be aware of what you say to yourself
and the impact on your perceptions,
emotions, and spirit.

Truth or Lies

"You're not good enough." "You should have done better." "You're stupid and lazy." After you've done a reality check and determined those words are not true, toss them out and replace them with positive, truthful ones. Negative, harsh, and even sarcastic words said in jest enter into our subconscious mind. If we allow them to settle and become part of our beliefs, we get stuck in a wilderness of feeling "less than" and inadequate. Self-check by asking Is there truth to what they said? Chapter 8 sheds insight on the truth of who you are.

I was helping to plan a party being held at a neighbor's home. I thought my ideas were good, and without realizing it I finagled for my plans to be accepted.

The party hostess yelled at me, "You are so controlling!"

A few not-so-nice words swirled in my head about what I thought of her. However, when I took the time to reflect on the planning process and our conversations, I realized she was right. I manipulated words and circumstances to get what I wanted.

I learned it's best to be verbally direct rather than manipulate people and conversations.

Speak the truth in love.

Honestly look at yourself and ask, "Are there valid reasons for what feels like their negative perception of me?"

Trying to control other people was affecting my relationships. I needed to recognize, take responsibility for, and receive counsel to get over that controlling nature. I'm still a bit of a "recovering controller," but I've learned to recognize it and realize I gain nothing by trying to control others or situations.

Someone throws shade at you. You're hurt and angry. Pause. Give it time and ask yourself objectively, "Is there any truth to what was said?" It may be challenging to look at ourselves objectively. So, before throwing shade back, consider asking someone you trust what they think about the situation. Then respond with facts and without name-calling, judgments, or criticism.

You're hurt by comments. What do you do?

1. Clarify with the speaker what you heard (reflective listening).

2. Assess the comments objectively (differentiate truth from lies).

3. Do nothing (forgive and let it go).
4. Ask a close friend if they see that undesirable characteristic in you.
5. Speak to the person and reconcile with them.

If what they said isn't true, don't let the lies settle in your head. I've actually said out loud, "I reject those words." Negative words are bad seeds planted in our brains, and at times we need to yell, "Crop failure!" sending them off to shrivel up.

Hopes, Dreams and Possibilities

With the world at your fingertips, it's easy to spend hours hopping between websites, videos, and emails. With all this media meandering, have you taken time to consider what you really want in life?

You have gifts, talents, and abilities with limitless possibilities. Yes. You! What are your strengths, interests, and passions? How can you use these to fulfill your hopes and dreams? What do you believe? "That will never happen?" or is it "I have a dream and goal for my life and will do what it takes (within boundaries) to fulfill them."

Write down your hopes, dreams, and goals to make them tangible and more attainable. Writing and also speaking out loud the desires of your heart are great first steps toward transforming dreams into reality.

Dream big because with God all things are possible, and the possibilities are limitless.

Communicating with Others

The self-talk tools also apply to talking with others. Since communication impacts every relationship, we'll take a deep dive here.

Communication is improved using a few simple tools. Whether communicating with friends, family, coworkers, or peers active listening is key. Focusing on and engaging with every speaker shows them we acknowledge what they are saying.

Active Listening Tools
Good
- ~ Mirror the speaker's body language (follow what they do)
- ~ Use eye contact
- ~ Smile when appropriate
- ~ Acknowledge their words with, "Uh-huh." "I see." "I get it." I know, right."
- ~ Ask questions

Not so good
- ~ Eye rolling
- ~ Grimacing
- ~ Smirking
- ~ Interrupting

Trusted Tool

Active listening indicates, "I value you and what you are saying."

A certain friend is an outstanding communicator. When we chat, I feel valued. I wondered why I felt that way. Then I realized she always asks questions about me and what I'm doing. When I speak, she looks me in the eye, nods her head, responds with affirmations, and asks follow-up questions. She shows genuine interest in what I say and in my life.

"How was the vacay? Heard you slayed the bike trail. Do you still like work? How did that appointment go?" Everyone has a story to tell, and most people like to tell their stories, but sometimes in a rush to tell our story, we forget to ask about theirs.

Active listening shows respect and genuine interest, leading to more meaningful and productive interactions and relationships.

Thoughts About the Other Person

You know that "preconceived notions" thing? Our perception about a person with whom we're communicating influences our conversations. Let's take a boss at work. Your last conversation ended with unresolved differing viewpoints, and you both got huffy. As you prepare for the next conversation consider how you will communicate. If you think your boss got over it you may not have any hesitation or anxiety in pursuing that next encounter. However, if you think they are still angry you might enter the conversation from a defensive posture.

What to do? Consider starting the conversation by verbalizing your preconceived notions. "Hey, the last time we spoke it seemed to me we were both a bit huffy. Are we good now?" Being open and up front clears the air for a better conversation.

Let's say you once had a conversation with someone who was critical and outright mean toward someone else. You're at a party and suddenly you're standing right next to that critical person. That last conversation left you uncomfortable, but not speaking would be super awkward. This might put you on the offense or defense, questioning if they might turn around and be critical of you.

The point is to check your perceptions of others with the reality of who they are. I've had bad days and made snarky remarks. Is that who I really am? No, but the person who was on the receiving end of my snarkiness might form that opinion of me. Enter into conversations without judgment, and at the same time understanding as much of their true nature as possible.

We spend 70 to 90 percent of our day engaged in some form of communication, with 55 percent of our time devoted to listening. Would you believe that our words only convey about 7 percent of what we're trying to say? The other 93 percent is communicated through facial expressions and the tone of our voice.[1]

During my many years of counseling, one day I had my own mic drop moment. I realized I wasn't listening during conversations. I knew how to talk it up, but when someone else was speaking, I was playing a chess game in my head planning my next verbal maneuver.

A counselor advised me, "Always focus on what the other person is saying, not on what you're going to say next."

Wow! During an argument, I was constantly strategizing my next response. I also realized even during a non-combative conversation I was thinking about what I was going to say next. I wasn't listening. One of the greatest gifts we give another person is listening to them and acknowledging what they've said.

Communication is as much about
our tone of voice, facial expressions,
and body language as it is about
our words.

Because a majority of communication is through body language we are constantly sending messages. Arms folded is the classic defensive position indicating that you don't agree or are protecting yourself. Resting your head on your hands at a table, even though you may simply be tired says that you're bored. Leaning forward is the posture of being engaged and listening.

Observing the body position of another person and subtly replicating their nonverbal signals and gestures is called mirroring. This technique helps to establish rapport, build trust, and create a sense of connection. If someone leans forward, you lean forward to show your attentiveness. If someone leans back in their chair they are saying, "I'm relaxed," and it is relational when you likewise do the same. Observing a person's facial expressions and body language gives you an idea of what's going on within them. Asking an appropriate question will facilitate further conversation.

Want people to listen? Open up your body language, smile, maintain eye contact, and use friendly gestures. Though we may not be fully cognizant of it, the thoughts we have during conversations are reflected in our words as well as in our body language.

When you're having "stinkin' thinkin'" be careful of what comes out of your mouth, as it might also be reflected in your body language. Recognize, be aware, and choose what messages you want to project.

Are the thoughts behind your words lending to uplifting communication or discouragement and enmity?

Positive Purpose, Positive Outcome

Establish a purpose when you begin a conversation.

1. Set the stage by speaking your intention and then listening to theirs.

2. Come into agreement about the purpose and desired outcome.

3. Keep aware and focused on the purpose for your conversation.

4. Reflectively listen and speak.

5. Tell stories to create visual imagery.

Hear with your mind *and* your heart what is being spoken. If what is said isn't clear, use reflective listening. Reflective listening is an essential communication tool. It requires actively listening and demonstrating understanding. It displays empathy by reflecting the speaker's thoughts, feelings, and experiences. A reflective listener uses such phrases as:

What I'm hearing you say is...

Did you say...?

I sense you are feeling...

It seems you are saying...

Would you please clarify?

Reflective listening is a great tool to avoid the communication wilderness! Repeating what we believe we've heard someone say and then acknowledging how they feel accomplishes much.

~ You, being the receiver, have the opportunity to momentarily process what's being said.

~ You can then repeat what you've heard.

~ The sender has an opportunity to hear in your words what you understood them to say.

~ Both parties are able to clarify the message.

Want to push someone's buttons—mine especially? Tell them what they're thinking and feeling when they don't think or feel that way. Ouch. For example, someone says to you, "You think I have all kinds of free time." They are perceiving through their own filters what they *believe* you are thinking or feeling. That is their reality. Though their perception is you think they have lots of free time and the reality is that's not what you think this is a great opportunity to say, "I heard you say you believe that I think you have all kinds of free time. Actually, that's not what I think. Tell me why you believe that please."

 **"Please let me clarify what I am really thinking."**

Acknowledging someone's feelings reflects empathy and compassion. When my parents were in the throes of a divorce. I understood it in my head, but my heart was tender. On a gray, snowy day Mom and I were in the car running errands. I sat quietly and pensively in the passenger seat. Discussing the divorce she said, "I know it hurts, honey. Go ahead and let it hurt." My pent-up emotions cut loose and I sobbed like a baby. With her words she acknowledged my sadness and pain. She allowed me to hurt, let me know it was okay to hurt, and helped me release the hurt.

 **A great gift! Relate in your heart and acknowledge with your words the feelings of others.**

At a marriage conference I grew weary hearing the facilitator tell so many stories. I wanted substance like how to improve communication and how to handle arguments. During the lunch break my husband surprisingly exclaimed how much he loved all the stories. At the close of the conference the facilitator explained that men especially effectively learn and remember through stories.

Stories using visual imagery engage our senses and emotions. Word pictures help listeners create images in their own minds, thus making them feel part of the story.

 Stories and visual imagery with our words enhance communication.

Communication Barriers

Anger, pride, and anxiety really mess with communication. If these are present it will be difficult to:

~ Connect verbally, emotionally, and mentally with others.

~ Express how you genuinely think and feel.

~ Communicate clearly.

Anger

Expressing anger constructively and appropriately is important for resolving conflicts and establishing healthy relationships. What's constructive and appropriate? Anger is a commonly expressed emotion. In and of itself it isn't bad, but what we *do* with that anger is either constructive or destructive. Anger affects the way our brain processes information at times making us illogical. When expressed through yelling and rage, others may end up feeling hurt, scared, and anxious.

"Getting your anger out" might make matters worse. Expressing anger is necessary, but is best handled using carefully chosen assertive words and not accusatory and violent words. Totally suppressing anger is unhealthy. Continually venting anger is also unhealthy. It's a delicate balancing act tempered by knowing our triggers and discerning when and how to express it.

Do people *make* us angry? Not so much. Remember, we acknowledge our perceptions, and we choose our thoughts and actions. We are responsible for our actions and words. Self-control is the difference between acting destructively in anger and responding calmly, constructively, and rationally. When angry we can use "I" statements to express feelings and thoughts without blaming or attacking others.

It's not true that if we don't act out the anger, we've given in, lost face, wimped out, or become a coward. Actually, the opposite is true. "It takes greater strength, self-restraint, introspection, and analysis to constructively resolve anger."[2]

The surface expression of anger masks other underlying emotions. Anger is often a surface emotion secondary to:

~ Loss
~ Guilt
~ Shame
~ Fear

Uncovering the core issues shoring up anger helps us learn to manage it. If it is a serious ongoing issue, a professional can help. I had two husbands with anger issues, both stemming from loss of identity, guilt and shame. When their anger triggered my anger our communication became a hot mess. I'm talking about anger where I had to leave the house because I couldn't control what was coming out of my own mouth.

I needed to deal with my own issues of control, fear, and anxiety. With the help of professionals and close friends we were able to uncover many of my secondary emotions and I was able to better manage my words and behavior.

Pride

Excessive pride, a.k.a. arrogance, involves an exaggerated sense of self-importance, inflated ego, and thinking one is superior to others. It's an attitude that oftentimes leads to a type of conduct. You've seen the scenario. You're at a gathering where someone is talking only about themselves. They're not necessarily an extrovert, they're just the person doing all the talking. A life coach might describe them as "sucking the air out of the room." Two potential reasons for this behavior might include: (1) excessive pride and (2) desire to control the conversation.

Aspects of pride include:
~ Concern about others' perceptions of us
~ Needing to find fault
~ Defensiveness
~ Need for attention
~ Desire to control others
~ Narcissism
~ Acknowledging people we perceive to be important and neglecting those we deem less important

People with the need to be right or speak the last word make communication difficult and create a barrier. Focusing on our own perspective and not listening shuts down communication. Listening takes into account other people's thoughts and opinions. When pride operates, only half the communication takes place. Recognizing pride is the first step to overcoming it. One of the most helpful pieces of advice I received in counseling is:

We don't have to like what someone says or like how they feel, but we are to listen to them and accept that this is their reality.

Anxiety

There is normal anxiety and then there's anxiety disorder. Normal anxiety presents as low levels of fear or apprehension not interfering with daily activities. Anxiety also causes foggy thinking and therefore we may not communicate well. The factors mentioned in Chapter 1 taking us into a wilderness season all have the potential to create anxiety. Within boundaries anxiety may actually improve one's attention and problem-solving ability and motivate one to work harder toward a goal. For example, anxiety about an upcoming exam or job interview could motivate someone to fully prepare. Normal anxiety could also be a warning about a potential threat.

Anxiety disorder, however, is an unusual level of anxiety that causes a decrease in performance and impairment. It involves an excessive persistent worry. If you struggle with persistent anxiety and worry, jump to page 113. You don't have to live with anxiety. Uncovering the cause is essential. I spent time with numerous secular and spiritual counselors when stressed and anxious. You too can conquer anxiety using *Trusted Tools*, including counseling.

When you recognize how anger, pride, and anxiety affect your communication, you've conquered a significant wilderness! Better communication. Better relationships. Better self-esteem.

Be Specific

Using pronouns instead of names causes confusion in conversations.

"I went to the party with Alex and Jessica, and we ran into Jacob and Kaitlyn. He said they went biking and she slayed the mountain course."

Who went biking? Alex or Jacob? Who are "they?" Who slayed the course, Jessica or Kaitlyn? Using names helps. Ask when you're not sure.

Hearing your name, spoken with affection, is one of the sweetest sounds to our ears and heart. Feel the difference between, "I appreciate you," versus "I appreciate you, Claire."

Alternatively, hearing your name in anger or with agitation doesn't feel so good.

 Use people's names with affection.

Clearing Communication Roadblocks

A close business associate and friend was working with me on an assignment. She said we would move forward when all materials arrived, which should be "any day." One, two, three days passed. I called and sent text messages to her. No response for two weeks. Each day I kept my schedule open so we could complete the assignment. I felt disrespected due to her lack of consideration for me and my time. After a month, still no materials. Therefore, I moved forward with someone else.

As a result of this experience she lost my trust and we didn't speak for a year. Eventually it dawned on me I had allowed unforgiveness to take hold. I needed to forgive her. Forgiveness is a somewhat complex subject and because it's so important I'll share a few basics.

Forgiveness

Unforgiveness ties you to another person with invisible shackles of thoughts and emotions. Forgiveness unlocks and releases you from harboring negative feelings and thoughts.

 Forgiving someone doesn't mean what they did was okay.

Forgiveness is an act of the heart and mind, which emotionally and spiritually releases us from that invisible tie to them or to the situation. For more on unforgiveness turn to page 73.

New Perceptions

In Chapter 2 we discussed perceptions and realities, which can be major barriers to communication. How do we form new perceptions? Look at a situation from the other person's perspective, from an outsider's perspective, or from God's perspective.

If your reality is consistent with the facts and you feel your perception is accurate, gently share that with the other person. Note the word *gently*. If you're perceiving one way and the other person is perceiving another way, use the reflective listening tools to clarify what each of you are saying to conquer this communication barrier.

Talk Instead of Text

Sounds radical, right? Run with me and let's unpack it. If 93 percent of our communication is facial expression and body language, how can we adequately communicate through text, email, and social media? Emojis? Well, maybe. We turn to little faces, icons, and memes to express ideas and feelings. And those little faces might make a big difference.

I already told you that.
vs
I already told you that.

A millennial friend said I use emojis too much. Probably true, but I want to express my feelings and intentions. The older people you know probably didn't grow up texting; we were tethered to a wall mounted phone by a cord! I sound like a dinosaur.

Of course, texting has great advantages. In seconds, we can accomplish what would take longer on a phone call. However, there are friends with whom I will seldom text because what they are trying to say is so confusing to me.

When we text, we know in our head what we're thinking, but it doesn't always come across exactly as intended. I sent a text to my friend Angela, telling her I met with our mutual friend.

> Angela: *Interesting, because she was supposed to be with us here in Detroit as our special speaker for our benefit dinner.*

> Me: *No way can she get away from the assignment she is on. It's totally covert. She mentioned Detroit and is sorry that she couldn't be there.*

> Angela: *Right.*

Right what? Was it sarcastic, meaning that's not true? Or "right" as in I'm familiar with her assignment? Had there been an emoji, maybe I would have known whether it was sarcasm or acknowledgement. Be specific. Be clear.

Another example: You get a text: *I can't be there by 5:30. I'll pick you up later.* When is later? 6:30? 8:30?

Or how about the word *soon*? To some people *soon* is five minutes and to others it's five hours. Watch for ambiguous words and be sure to *clarify.*

About	He
However	I'll try
In a few	Kind of
Later	She
Soon	Sort of
Stuff	They
Whatever	When I can
Whenever	Whichever
Whoever	

Electronic communications are part of life, and sometimes an old-fashioned phone call, face-to-face live media, or an in-person conversation are necessary for full expression. When possible, emotionally charged topics, such as relationships, job changes, or illness, warrant a live conversation.

At the same time, written words—whether in a text, email, or letter—when well worded may be clearer and more succinct. And remember what mama said, "Don't put anything in writing you don't want the whole world to see!" *How* we communicate, through a device or in person, is as important as *what* we communicate.

My favorite questions to bring clarity are:

~ Do you want me to respond to what you said or just listen? (I frequently start with this one)

~ Have you considered . . . ?

~ Have you thought of . . . ?

~ Would it be helpful to . . . ?

Harness Your Tongue

"Death and life are in the power of
the tongue." (Proverbs 18:21)

In numerous relationships, I was at fault in an argument. I reacted all over the place with harsh words. Okay, I was pretty good at arguing. But good in the fight didn't make me feel good in my heart—and not proud of it.

To have harmony in relationships I had to learn how to harness my tongue; to control what feisty Lana was going to blurt out versus what I was actually going to say. It's taken years of practice and still does! It's important to carefully choose the words we speak, and helpful to be aware of the many factors influencing what we say.

The Five Cs of Communication

Clear, Concise Communication
Creates Clarity

What's in the Way of Productive Communication?

We consist of a soul (our mind, will and emotions) and spirit, all existing in our physical body. See the diagram on page 60. They are all integrated. When one is out of whack another will be affected, and they *all* influence our thoughts and feelings thus influencing our communication. Let's clear it up.

What's Clouding Your Filter? The Present

My communication filter became pretty gunked up over the years, and I was not a great communicator. Eventually I came to recognize how when one of these influencers (body, soul and spirit) got out of alignment my communication was clouded.

In addition, such factors as my previous life experiences, concerns about my future, my upbringing, current and past physical conditions, and current and past relationships all contributed to tough times of communication.

Physical Body

We have more than one hundred trillion cells in our bodies, making up the eleven major systems of our body:

1. Integumentary
2. Skeletal
3. Muscular
4. Nervous
5. Endocrine
6. Cardiovascular
7. Lymphatic

8. Respiratory
9. Digestive
10. Urinary
11. Reproductive

Foods & Beverages

All of these systems were created to function in sync. That's the ideal, but it doesn't always work that way. When one system gets out of balance, it can trigger others to get out of balance. From personal experience I can attest that food and beverages significantly affect the words coming out of our mouths.

One evening at a restaurant I enjoyed a delicious dinner with a wine-cherry-mushroom sauce covering the entrée. The next day I was a mess: tired, unmotivated, and my emotions were raw and irritable. I cried throughout the day and couldn't keep a single positive thought in my brain. I said out loud, "I just want this day to end, so I can get up tomorrow feeling better."

What happened? Though I had not previously experienced a mushroom allergy there is a family history of such, and most likely I had an allergic reaction. So what did I do that day? As little as possible, and I should have kept my lips zipped. During several phone conversations I got emotionally worked up and started crying. Definitely, wisdom would say to have those calls another time. I tried to read and listen to uplifting, positive media, but the funk was so deep even that didn't help. The lesson? If I must have a serious or important conversation, I have to be cognizant of how I am feeling physically and emotionally.

 ### When you don't feel well, consider rescheduling important discussions.

Perhaps it wasn't the mushrooms; the funky reaction could have been from the wine sauce. According to *Medical News Today,* as soon as alcohol enters the bloodstream the brain is affected. This information is personal to me for several reasons: (1) the worst arguments in my life happened when I had been drinking, (2) my youngest brother died of alcoholic liver disease, and (3) now after I have even a little bit of alcohol, I am so cranky and tired the next day; I can barely tolerate myself!

No judgments here. After all, Jesus' first miracle was turning water into wine. Some people can drink with no side effects the next day, and having a little nip for some gives what I call, "A brain vacation." However, if you need or desire alcohol every day, please reach out to a professional. See the resources at the end of the book.

 ### Avoid important conversations and making major decisions if drinking, taking heavy medications, or either person doesn't feel well.

What about the "feel good" foods and beverages? Ah yes, those yummy sugary treats make our taste buds and emotions jump with glee. Unfortunately, sugar is rough on our bodies.

Chocolate is known for having a high number of antioxidants, and I've learned to avoid the super sugary ones. I make my own dark chocolate treat sweetened with honey or maple syrup. Other feel-good foods are salmon, berries, olive oil, walnuts, flaxseed, bananas and leafy greens. Try a few and see what works for you.

Allergies and Environment

I waited until my son, Alex, was two and a half before giving him red watermelon–flavored gelatin. I remember it well. Within minutes he spun circles in the kitchen yelling, "Mommy, help me! Mommy, help me!" I was stunned and sickened. What did I do to this sweet child? I wrapped my arms around him and held him tightly until he calmed down. We observed similar behavior every time he ate anything with red dye. Allergy testing indicated that red dye 40 was the culprit.

Physical and chemical reactions in our brain affect our emotions, words, and actions.

Traditional doctors tested him for allergies and the effects of their recommendations were minimal. They suggested medications to alleviate the symptoms, but didn't address the source of the issues. When Alex was four, while visiting family out of town he suddenly began gasping for air. When your kid is struggling to breathe, the panic is like no other. We rushed him to the family allergist, who stabilized his breathing with inhalers.

He had had an asthma attack accompanied by an infection and fever. The doctor prescribed five medications. Seriously! *Five* medications for a four-year-old.

Being a first-time mom, I followed doctor's orders. After three days of being loaded up with all the drugs, he was wild! This normally well-behaved, sweet little guy went zonkers. He was uncooperative, yelling at everyone, and crying a lot. By now I was crying a lot too. At times nothing could calm him. After one particularly erratic morning of dealing with my inconsolable kid, I was so emotionally drained I needed a few minutes alone. How's that for a mom who dearly loves her child? Wisdom is knowing when to stay and when to go.

Alex was settled and watching TV so I ran upstairs to his walk-in closet. I shut the door and got down on my knees. I'll remember that moment forever. With tears streaming down my cheeks, I reached into the air with my right hand, and in my mind's eye I saw a rope. I thought of the saying, "When you reach the end of your rope, tie a knot in it and hang on." I said out loud, "Lord! I am at the end of my rope! I will never put my child on five medications again. You've got to show me another way."

Yes, I told God he *had* to do something—and He did.

My knotted-up, stressed-out body needed my chiropractor. She asked what was going on. I told her about Alex's allergies, illnesses, and medications. Being a holistic chiropractor, she recommended an environmental medicine doctor. I immediately scheduled an appointment.

During our first visit, Alex behaved wonderfully while the doctor and I discussed his medical history. It was late in the morning, and I gave him what I thought was a healthy snack. After chowing down his sandwich, he began to tug on computer cords, wouldn't listen, and was acting out—very different behavior than when we first arrived.

The doctor kindly said, "I can see something has set him off."

"What do you mean?" I asked.

She said, "The first place we have an allergic reaction is in our brains. We ingest foods and almost immediately, the brain responds."

She further explained the correlation between foods and beverages, and the interaction in the brain leading to behavioral changes. I started to cry. Finally! I had an answer as to how my loving, sweet boy at the flip of a switch (or flip of a food) could become totally out of control.

My prayer was heard and answered. That wilderness season led to this mom becoming well educated in food, chemical, and environmental sensitivities. Upon further testing, we learned Alex was allergic to forty things including dust, molds, dyes, trees, and grasses.

An extremely challenging wilderness often leads to a purposeful outcome.

Seeing such great results with Alex on antigens to counteract the allergies, I inquired about my own health. She diagnosed me with mercury toxicity consistent with industrial exposure. Bottom line—Alex's allergies led us to a caring holistic medical doctor, and the discovery of me having mercury toxicity.

Know which foods, beverages, and other triggers lead to undesirable mental and emotional responses in yourself and in those around you!

Time for a Public Service Announcement (PSA). If you, your children, or other family members experience physical, mental, or emotional issues, a productive first step is to remove all scented products from your home such as: cleaning supplies, laundry detergents, dryer sheets (many have formaldehyde), perfumes, colognes, scented candles, and air fresheners. A study by the University of Melbourne found that "98.5 per cent of us are exposed to fragranced products on a daily or weekly basis and although they may smell good or clean, they may be making us sick."[3]

A particular perfume literally sends me into la-la-land! When exposed to it my brain immediately goes haywire. Many perfumes, colognes, and scented products cause congestion and brain dysfunction. Remember, a first reaction is in our brain. Check your home and be considerate of others. Brain fog definitely lands us in a communication wilderness.

Also consider what scents and chemicals are present outside the home; daycare, schools, work, and frequently visited places where chemicals may be used. Exposure to chemicals in these places can result in physical, psychological, and emotional responses as well.

What does all of this have to do with communication? Everything! If our brain isn't functioning well, our communication isn't functioning well.

How do you know if you're affected? Being aware that foods, beverages, and the environment can trigger mental, emotional, and physical responses. Please, take time to observe and consider whether any of these might be affecting you and those around you.

Fatigue and Lack of Sleep

I am a total foggy head when I don't sleep enough. A holistic doctor asked how my sleep hygiene was. Say what? As a former dental hygienist, *hygiene* to me meant cleaning teeth. She explained that sleep hygiene is a "clean" environment conducive to sleep before and while you're sleeping. Creating a hygienic sleep environment includes:

~ Avoiding stimulants (caffeine, alcohol) too close to bedtime.

~ Avoiding fatty, fried, heavy, or spicy meals right before bed.

~ Avoiding electronic devices with bright screens.

~ Establishing a regular bedtime routine.

~ Keeping the room as dark as possible.

Sleep well, be well!

Depression

Just as numerous factors affect our sleep, other tangible factors can have adverse physical, mental, and emotional responses, and even cause depression. These include:

~ Environment
~ Medications
~ Hormones
~ Vitamin and mineral deficiencies

Depression is another animal altogether. After diagnosing a low hormone level, my doctor prescribed a hormone replacement. Five days later I was crying all day, and positive thoughts were elusive. I wondered if it was depression. I had never experienced such a deep endless lethargy and sadness. My doctor adjusted the dosages and the symptoms faded away.

I gained tremendous empathy for those in a depression wilderness. Depression symptoms include overwhelming sadness, low energy, loss of appetite, and a lack of interest in things that used to bring pleasure.[4] If you think you're depressed, explore the above influences, consider the physical triggers you suspect might be a problem, and consider what you might change. If depression symptoms persist, seek professional counsel.

Trusted Tool

Medications, environment, and vitamin and mineral deficiencies potentially affect our bodies, our thinking, and our communication.

Physical Illnesses and Injuries

Illness and injuries can result in pain, loneliness, and isolation, which in turn impact our thoughts, emotions, and therefore our communication. Frustration, discouragement, and disappointment set in when we can't walk, work, or do simple daily tasks. We may have to depend on others for help.

A friend was dealing with horrible pain. Much of the time she was angry, worried, and irrational. Being around her was like walking through a landmine—I never knew when she would verbally explode. One day in a counseling course I was taking I had an aha moment. The instructor said, "People who are in pain are very likely to exhibit symptoms of depression." Immediately I understood that my friend was suffering with depression because of the pain and she lashed out because of it.

Perceptions, thoughts, emotions, and behaviors are affected by medications, hormones, allergies, our environment, past experiences, and current circumstances. When communication gets tough, keep in mind your communication *Trusted Tools* when speaking and listening.

Mind, Will, Emotions and Heart

In addition to how our physical body influences our communication, we'll now consider the influence of our soul. Body, soul, and spirit affect perceptions of yourself and others, and even your possibilities. Each part of you affects other parts. Body, soul, and spirit are all integrated.

1. We have a body—our physical being.

2. We have a soul—our mind, will, and emotions.

3. We have a spirit—the part of us connected to a higher dimension, to God.

Some use the terms *soul* and *spirit* interchangeably. For this discussion we are a combination of body, soul, and spirit plus the heart. All are interconnected and together influence our perceptions.

Knowing how we're designed and what makes us tick, equips us to get through the wilderness—and all of life. Perceptions are key as we enter into and out of wilderness seasons, and to understanding what happens while we're there. My wilderness seasons would have been a lot less stressful had I understood the interconnection between my thoughts, my physical body, my emotions, and my spirit. I don't have regrets, though, because I learned and grew through those seasons as I still do every day.

Perceptiveness of our body, soul, and spirit is essential to making good choices as we conquer the wilderness.

As a teenager, I received a copy of the *Optimist Creed* from Optimist International. Reading it made me feel, well, optimistic. At that time, the insights from the Optimist Creed, along with what I learned in church, became my moral compasses. When I felt pressured or worried, I was encouraged by these concepts and felt hopeful. Today, my most Trusted Tool is God's Word. In it is every answer to every question in life. I rely on it daily for wisdom, encouragement, and support.

Mind

What we read, watch, and listen to goes into our conscious and subconscious mind. Volumes of information exist on how we think. How and what we think is imperative to understanding wilderness seasons.

Several influencers of our thoughts are:
- ~ What we view on our phones, computers, and TV.
- ~ What we listen to including music, people, and news.
- ~ What we read.
- ~ Our current and past experiences.
- ~ Our current lifestyle, job, and relationship situations.

We are what we read, watch, listen to, and think.

Everything we look at and listen to becomes part of our thought process. What we allow into our heads through our eyes and ears becomes integrated into our thoughts, our emotions, and thereby influences our responses.

"If you don't like your thought, have another one!" (Graham Cooke)

In the wilderness, our perceptions and mental processing can deceive us into thinking what we see is all there is. If exposed to negativity, we may feel down, distracted, and disappointed. When exposed to positive and uplifting influences and environments, we're inclined to feel encouraged, happy, and hopeful.

One evening I watched a movie featuring a mountaintop home with breathtaking scenes overlooking the sparkling turquoise waters of the Mediterranean Sea. Vines of red flowers cascaded over the trellis hugging the house. Through the night, as I periodically awakened my mind replayed the beautiful scenery from the movie. I slept ten hours that night.

Good stuff in, good stuff out.

Will

Our will is a complex subject, so here it is simplified; it is our capacity to make conscious choices and decisions, and to act on them. We have desires and we make choices. However, during a wilderness season, there may be extenuating circumstances which create difficulty in making reasonable choices.

The abuse Lance endured tied his soul into a controlling addiction to pornography. His will was to be a good, kind, and loving person. But the addiction overpowered his will, and at times he was mean, angry, and abusive. We have choices, and it takes courage and at times professional help to make choices in the best interest of ourselves and others. A courageous act of our will may be the choice to seek help from professionals.

Acknowledge your desires, intentions, and motivations. Be aware of how these guide and influence your choices and actions.

Emotions

We explored emotions relevant to our physical selves, now let's dig a little deeper.

We're real, and we feel. All day long we feel something. We feel good when things go well; we feel down when things don't go well. We're happy, and we're sad. We have patience, and we're impatient. We have courage, and we are afraid. Emotions are triggered when we lose a relationship, marriage, job, loved one, pet, or material object.

Unreconciled emotions impact our health and ability to communicate. If feelings and emotions are not recognized and understood, we tend to react rather than respond. Our emotions and reactions are influenced by our past experiences and by how we've been taught or not taught to handle them. Who taught us to deal with the emotions surrounding loss? Were we held in a parent's arms and told to go ahead and cry, or were we told to buck up and get over it? What did we learn from observing others as they dealt with loss?

Answers to these questions are essential to navigating an emotional wilderness. My first husband and I went through counseling for ten years before we divorced. Yes, ten years and six counselors, and still the marriage didn't work out. In nearly every session the counselor asked how I felt. Sometimes I had no idea. It took a chart with feeling words to help. Here is a partial list.

HAPPY	SAD	ANGRY	OTHER FEELINGS
Calm	Ashamed	Annoyed	Afraid
Cheerful	Awful	Bugged	Anxious
Confident	Disappointed	Destructive	Ashamed
Content	Discouraged	Disgusted	Bored
Delighted	Gloomy	Frustrated	Confused
Excited	Hurt	Fuming	Curious
Glad	Lonely	Furious	Embarrassed
Loved	Miserable	Grumpy	Jealous
Proud	Sorry	Irritated	Moody
Relaxed	Unhappy	Mad	Responsible
Satisfied	Unloved	Mean	Scared
Silly	Withdrawn	Violent	Shy
Terrific			Uncomfortable
Thankful			Worried

If getting in touch with your emotions is painful, or you begin to feel overwhelmed, call a close friend and share what's going on, or consider the counseling suggestions at the end of the book. Understanding how we feel helps us:

~ Communicate more effectively,

~ Respond authentically instead of reacting from negative emotions, and

~ Create a more harmonious atmosphere around us.

We think with our mind, we act from our will, and we feel with our emotions. Every action we take, every word we say, and every emotion we feel is a result of how and what we think.

Understanding how our mind, will and emotions influence our thinking is crucial to having hope in wilderness seasons.

Heart

At a conference the speaker said, "Put your hand on your heart." All around the room people moved their hands to their chests. The speaker said, "Okay, that's your physical heart. Your other heart is here," and he put his hand on his head. The heart is more than something with which we feel; it represents our spiritual thoughts and desires. "As [a person] thinks in [their] heart, so is he [or she]" (Proverbs 23:7 NLT).

Perhaps we tell people we love them "with all our heart," conveying we love them with our whole being. Think of the heart as the core of our spiritual, intellectual, emotional, and moral activity. It functions as part of our conscience and drives our actions, words, and behavior. "Out of the abundance of the heart, the mouth speaks" (Matthew 12:34 ESV).

What's Clouding Your Filter? The Past

Without realizing it, buried emotions and painful past events can and do cloud your communication filter. The information in the previous section is important, and now let's go a bit further and explore how the past can affect us in ways we may not realize.

At a marriage conference the facilitator said, "Whether you stay married or not depends on how you learn to fight." Those words actually upset me. For me, fighting and arguing frequently resulted in hurt feelings, and no resolution to the argument. I figured, "Why fight? Someone is going to get hurt."

Heated discussions and differing opinions exist no matter what. So what do we do?

Recognize pain, hurt, and trauma from the past. Acknowledge the effect and connection to our current communication style.

First Communication

From the time we're born we communicate. At first we squeak, cry, smile, and babble. Then we model our parents, grandparents, or guardians, and sometimes even what is viewed on social media and television. When effective communication is modeled for us, chances are we will communicate well. If it isn't, then we need to work at improving our communication skills. Take a dive into how you learned to communicate growing up.

A big cloud to my communication filter was criticism. I grew up around a lot of it. Looking back, I now see because of my parents' un-healed hearts and souls they were critical. "You don't do enough." "Why the *#&@ did you park the car there?" Growing up with criticism, I became critical of myself and others—a really bad thought process and resulting behavior pattern. I then married my first husband who truly believed criticism was a way to get someone to improve their behavior and character. No kidding. Verbal fireworks blew up when his critical words pushed my old "fear of criticism" and "self-critical" buttons. When I eventually learned to listen to my self-talk and heard the negative stuff I was saying to myself, I was able to reprogram my thoughts and stop being critical of myself and of others.

To this day, I listen to my own thoughts and am intentionally aware of not criticizing myself and others.

Intentionality is a *Trusted Tool* for conquering a communication wilderness.

Trauma, Abuse, PTSD

Trauma and post-traumatic stress disorder (PTSD) may stem from emotional, physical, or sexual abuse. PTSD can follow an accident or injury, major surgery or illness, death of loved one, natural disasters, and war to name a few. The short and long-term effects of trauma can hang on until we recognize it and talk about it.

The short- and long-term effects of trauma in the mind and emotions are real, albeit in the intangible category as mentioned in Chapter 1. For example, even though we can't physically touch them, the memories and emotions of the day a loved one died are very real.

Painful memories may flicker and crackle at times. I couldn't fix them like I could replace a broken light bulb. The memories stored in my brain at one time affected every part of my being.

My soul, spirit and heart carried trauma until I identified it and dealt with it. I recognized it and saw the effects it was having on me. I knew I had to deal with it. And now you can too.

Hurting people hurt people—often with words.

Emotional outbursts, extreme anger, aggressive behavior, withdrawal, addiction, persistent difficulty sleeping, problems at work or school, and relationship challenges describe common manifestations of trauma. If you've experienced any kind of trauma and you can't stop thinking about it, please seek professional help. This wilderness season requires help to get you through. If you recognize any of these behaviors in yourself, consult with a family member, trusted friend, a professional or spiritual counselor, and act now. There are resources at the end of this book to guide you.

When someone is in a deep state of grief or trauma, recounting your personal traumatic experience can be emotional overload. Sometimes you may help another person by relating your own experience, but I found when I was in my own state of grief it wasn't helpful. After my husband's suicide, well-intended people started sharing their own stuff, and it got to the point where I had to say, "I'm sorry. I really can't hear that right now." I felt a bit uncomfortable shutting them down, but ultimately setting this healthy emotional boundary was best for me.

A dear friend and I conversed months after Lance's Celebration of Life service. I asked if she was there. She kindly responded, "Yes. Don't you remember? We chatted in the hallway for about five minutes?" Until she reminded me, I had no recollection of the conversation. We're not as sharp during a state of trauma.

Fear

Fear is an emotional response to a perceived threat or danger. It may evolve from trauma relevant to an accident, injury, abuse, loss, illness, the unknown, and more. It can be triggered by real threats or imagined ones. Feeling fearful may be a natural protective response, but excessive or persistent fear that interferes with daily life may be indicative of an anxiety disorder. What can we do? I experienced this dilemma myself many times, and each time made a choice.

I drove my friend to an appointment. While pulling into a parking space, I fully believed I had at least six inches of clearance from the yellow divider pole. Suddenly an awful screech pierced our ears. I rammed the car right into that yellow pole. My friend jumped out and yelled, "Get out and look." Silly girl. I couldn't get out. My door was jammed against the pole. There was only one thing to do. I had to back out even though it further damaged the car.

I didn't really care for the new yellow striping on my burgundy car, but I caused the accident so what could I do? Getting mad at myself wasn't useful or productive. I made an error in judgment and that was it. I was quite calm and simply said, "Thank goodness for car insurance."

I plodded through the steps to get the car repaired, but here's what surprised me. For the next week, each time I pulled into or out of a parking space, I was really nervous. One day after parking my car, I called my sister. I shared with her that since the accident, I was anxious when parking.

She said, "You have PTSD!"

As soon as she said it, I realized she was right. Without recognizing it, I was having a post-traumatic response to a minor, no-injury episode with a stationary pole!

Now that I understood why I was feeling anxious, I gradually got over it by telling myself when parking, "I am good at parking." Also, I became more attentive and aware.

Not having fear is possible when we turn to the highest source in the universe—God.

My many years in counseling gave me a better idea of how to deal with fear. Here are a few lessons I learned which I pass along to help you too.

First, acknowledge and take time to understand the feelings surrounding whatever led to the pain, injury, illness, or accident that is causing the fear. Refer back to the feelings chart on page 65. Are you angry, sad, frustrated, or annoyed?

Second, once you understand how you feel about a situation, the next step is to identify what is triggering those feelings. Were feelings triggered by a past occurrence or a current situation? Are your perceptions based on the reality of the situation? Is your overall physical and emotional health being affected?

For me, I couldn't change the traumas that occurred, so I knew I needed to chill over it. But I also needed to acknowledge my trigger-related feelings and the fear connected to them. I recall an earlier time in life when I was fearful. I missed an entire month of middle school. Sick at home my throat felt like sandpaper was rubbing it raw and the pain was accompanied with extreme fatigue. Yes, those are symptoms of mononucleosis, a.k.a. mono. Regardless of how much I slept, I was incessantly exhausted all the while trying to keep up with schoolwork. Prolonged anxiety about my incomplete study assignments triggered negative, fearful emotions as I felt pressured to stay caught up.

When the car incident happened, I recognized those same feelings of middle school fear and the pattern I had carried with me. It wasn't quite the same fear, but I was afraid of what might happen next.

Emotions are real. But remember from Chapter 2 to fact check them with reality. Recognizing emotional triggers helps us approach situations with more clarity. When I had mono, had my feelings not ruled, I would have suffered less stress over the incomplete schoolwork. Anxiety is counterintuitive to our being and healing. Now, things have changed for me as I have learned to handle those feelings differently. I flip from anxious and stressful thoughts to thoughts of, "I will do the best I can. That's the best I can do."

I've been able to pass on some of this wisdom to my son. Alex, a lover of extreme sports, has had many accidents, injuries, and illnesses growing up. After missing practices or games he would yell or slam a door in frustration and then withdraw with disappointment. He would let his feelings out, but he didn't let them rule. He ultimately would say, "There's nothing I can do about it, so I won't dwell on it." Through the disappointments he recognized and accepted the circumstances he couldn't change.

When we redirect our focus from negative to positive thoughts it ultimately influences our emotions. We can choose to accept our situation or reject and fight against it. Choosing is a decision, an act of our will. Acceptance of an accident or occurrence doesn't imply a lack of desire to overcome the difficulty. It means we acknowledge the circumstance for what it is, and we use our *Trusted Tools* to work with the circumstance not against it.

Acknowledge. Accept. Advance.

Unforgiveness

We've all been hurt by someone. When we see them, or if their name comes up and our blood begins to boil, we're holding on to unforgiveness. Are you harboring anger or resentment toward someone who hurt you?

I asked a trusted friend, an accomplished businessman, what he thought about me making a particular financial decision. He gave his advice relevant to the current economic climate and I followed his directive. Years later, when my monthly cash flow was messed up, I realized had I *not* followed his advice I wouldn't have had a cash flow crunch. There were lots of tears. There was more counseling. There were many prayer calls with trusted friends. I knew I had to move forward and forgive him and myself. Yes, it was my decision to follow his suggestion, but I still resented the situation and his advice. Not a good place to be.

Unforgiveness had become a stone wall around my mind and heart. It kept inside me the negative emotions which were screaming to get out and to be released. I knew the only way to free my heart was to tear down the wall of bondage and to forgive. It wasn't easy. I repeatedly said, "I forgive him."

After lots of mental gymnastics I realized: (1) I asked his opinion, (2) he gave what he thought was good advice, and (3) I made the best decision I could at the time. Later, when I realized it was not the best decision, I knew I had to forgive the friend, forgive myself, accept the circumstance, and move on.

Then there was the time I had a beautiful sparkling glass top dining table delivered to my home. After the delivery men left, I noticed a chip on the table. The owner of the delivery company paid me only a fraction of the cost of replacing the glass. Every time I see that chip it reminds me to forgive.

Forgiveness doesn't release someone from their wrong actions. Forgiving an individual doesn't mean what they did was okay. This is especially true with physical or sexual abuse. I repeat, forgiveness does not release someone from the responsibility of their actions. Forgiveness sets *us* free because it's a decision of our will. We decide to say, "I forgive them."

These words don't come easy because they oppose our flesh—our mind and emotions. What helped me to forgive my businessman friend was to speak the words "I forgive him" into the atmosphere. Eventually forgiveness settled in my heart. Also, it can start in our heart and then settle in our mind and emotions.

Speaking to a person face to face is very powerful. I was in my thirties when I said to my father, "I forgive you for abusing the family the way you did."

He was genuinely surprised. He didn't deny the abuse, but truly had difficulty recalling his actions. When I shared specifics, he apologized. This face-to-face conversation and act of forgiveness took down heart-barriers and brought a lightness to both of our souls and spirits.

The starting place with forgiveness—is forgiving ourselves! Let that settle for minute. We've all made mistakes, decisions we regret, and have done stupid things. Stop beating yourself up! Say to yourself, "I forgive me!" I forgive myself for listening to that advice. I forgive myself for lashing out with horrible words. Making things right with others may not be easy, but you'll be freer when you do.

Some of the most powerful words in the world are "I'm sorry. Will you forgive me?"

Communication Triggers

Triggers are what we smell, see, hear, touch, or experience that activate an emotion followed by a reaction. Triggers arise from our prior experiences. Much of this was covered in Chapter 1 and here are a few specifics.

Lance's physical and emotional trauma filters significantly affected our communication. Frequently, what he *thought* I had said made him explode. He became defensive and went on a verbal attack toward me. When I tried to clarify and repeat word for word exactly what I said, he still didn't get it. He would repeat what he *thought* I said; it wasn't even close. This was a super frustrating wilderness landscape.

In previous relationships I was afraid to ask for what I wanted and needed for fear of being turned down. I didn't want to be rejected. In this new marriage I made an effort to express my desires and needs. When Lance arrived home after work, I liked being greeted with a hello, a hug, or some form of acknowledgement. Instead, he would walk in the door and run straight upstairs to his office.

One day I said, "It would mean a lot to me when you come home if you acknowledged me with a hello, a hug, or something."

He said, "You're always telling me I don't do enough."

Bam! What? When I expressed a desire important to me, because of his personal filter—cloudy due to childhood and adult traumas—what he heard was me being critical of him. The conversation might have gone better this way:

> Me: "It would mean a lot to me if when you come home, you acknowledge me with a hello, or a hug, or something."
>
> Him: "So you want me to say hello or acknowledge you when I get home?"
>
> Me: "Yes."
>
> Him: "Well, I don't really feel like saying hello or anything. When I get home, I want to be alone and decompress."

In this scenario, there is no finger pointing, no accusations, no defensive kickback. He wanted one thing, and I wanted another. In that case whose need gets met? Will I acknowledge and accept his desire to be alone? Ideally further discussion would take place.

Here's where it gets sticky. We all have personal filters. Everything that has happened to us in our lives, every experience, every word, and every situation is in our memory bank. Our thoughts and perceptions are filtered through all of this and affect our communication. Be aware of perceptions and assumptions. Let's not assume someone has heard us correctly.

Clarifying what we've said improves communication.

At a happy hour gathering a woman approached me. She never introduced herself, but instead for a full five minutes cursed and berated my friend. I had never heard such vitriol in my life.

As she continued ranting, I asked myself, "Do I tell her how this person is a dear friend to me and how he was there for me at a critical time in my life? Do I keep quiet?" I decided to say nothing.

However, after the encounter I wondered if I should have said something or if I did the right thing by saying nothing. I asked a trusted friend (there's wisdom in a multitude of counselors). She wisely said, "Anything you would have said at that point would have been fuel to fire."

Our silence can speak volumes.

Cleaning Your Filter

Counseling

Messy perceptions and mental filters make communication challenging, therefore counseling with a mental health or spiritual health professional often provides helpful insight to clean things up.

Recent Barna data states, "Americans by far have positive experiences with counseling—a practice that helps them heal from trauma, facilitate mental health, build strong relationships and change destructive patterns of thinking" (BarnaTrends

HE SAID, SHE SAID, I SAID

2018, Baker Books).

- ~ 42% of adults have seen a counselor at some point in their lives.
- ~ 13% say they are currently seeing a counselor or therapist.
- ~ 28% say they've seen a counselor or therapist in the past.
- ~ 36% say they're at least open to it.
- ~ 23% say they would never see a counselor.

By comparison:
- ~ 21% of millennials and 16% of gen Xers are currently engaged in therapy.
- ~ 8% of boomers and 1% of the elderly are presently working with a counselor or therapist.

As mentioned, my first husband and I received counseling from six professionals over ten years. I needed to know we had given the marriage everything we could. Though we divorced, the lessons learned through counseling were applicable to all relationships, my family, and myself.

Years later, through deeper spiritual counseling and prayer, the core wounds in my life were further uncovered. With help I was able to let go of past generational wounds and release myself and others from past mistakes and traumas. Only then was I able to be scrubbed clean of my past dirt and healed from the inside out. (If you can't wait to read how, jump to chapters 7 and 8.)

Effective Communication
- ~ Like mama said, "Think before you speak."
- ~ Tell the truth.
- ~ Let others speak; be a good listener.
- ~ Respect others' viewpoints.
- ~ Be open about your feelings with others and yourself.
- ~ Ask for what you want, desire, and need without being manipulative with your words.
- ~ Listen to your self-talk.
- ~ Avoid making assumptions about other's thoughts, feelings, and behavior.
- ~ Clarify.
- ~ Enhance your own communications through active and reflective listening.

The Most Important Conversation You'll Have All Day!

One of the most important things I hope you get out of this book is that we are all loved. I am loved. You are loved. It's true! No matter what we've done or what we've said, we can be forgiven. We are loved, and the One who loves us speaks to us. This leads to the ultimate form of communication: talking with the Divine, talking with God.

The human soul and spirit thrive on love.

A well-known talk show co-host once mocked a public figure for saying Jesus talks to him. The co-host said, "It's one thing to talk to Jesus. It's another thing when Jesus talks to you. That's called mental illness if I'm not correct." This caused a national uproar. Perhaps the host's perspective was based on her personal life and choices. If she didn't believe in God or Jesus, then from her point of reference how could anyone hear from them? So what was she suggesting? Was it okay to talk to a divine being, but not okay to hear from them?

There is nothing in the world that humbles me, amazes me, and flips my switch like the fact—yes, it's a fact—that the Divine Creator of the universe wants to talk with us. How cool is that! God wants to talk to us, and we can hear His voice. We can chat it up with ourselves and with other people, but talking with God is the most important communication in the world. How important? All of Chapter 7 is dedicated to it, so if you can't wait to hear the good news jump there now.

"Call to Me and I will answer you, and tell you great and mighty things, which you do not know." (Jeremiah 33:3 ESV)

TOOLBOX

◻ What people or events from your past
  or in your present sphere influence your
  communication filter? Reflect on significant
  events influencing your communication style.

◻ Think about a super challenging
  communication—let's call it what it is,
  an argument or fight. What triggered the
  argument? Without using the words *he*, *she*
  or *they said*, identify the personal triggers that
  set you off and made you say things you wish
  you hadn't.

◻ For the next twenty-four hours listen to what
  you think about and what you say to yourself.
  Yes! Think about what you're thinking. Are
  you hearing, "That was so stupid," or are you
  hearing, "I'll do better next time?"

◻ How can you encourage yourself? "I did a
  good job at that. I'm going to have a great
  day. I can do this!" What are other things you
  can tell yourself?

◻ Is your self-talk making you feel stressed and
  depressed or encouraged and uplifted?

CHAPTER 4

Dealing With Loss

We live our lives; we experience loss. Loss is part of life. From my experience, the same factors affecting our communication—food, environment, health, thoughts, and perceptions—also impact how we process loss.

Processing loss is important because burying your feelings and not processing the grief leads to stress, depression, anxiety, lashing out, and other undesirable behaviors. It affects our physical body's health, as well as our mind and spirit. So how do we deal with loss? There's a lot of help in this toolbox!

Managing Loss and Grief

Whether we've lost a pet, a person, or a plan for our future, loss leads to a wilderness landscape. To deal with this wilderness, *Trusted Tools* are essential. Loss affects our emotions, our thinking, and our spiritual being.

In Chapter 1 we touched on tangible and intangible losses, and in Chapter 3 we explored the body, soul, and spirit connections. Navigating loss is a subject that could take up an entire book, so I'll pull together what we've previously covered with the addition of a few basic tools.

Personal Relationships

In a new marriage a couple typically brings together their individual hopes, dreams, and visions of a wonderful, shared life. However, if communication goes south the marriage may become a challenging wilderness.

One of my marriages ended in divorce and the other in suicide. There were many wonderful times and also painful wilderness times. When I say wilderness times, I'm not talking about some three-day mountain hike for which you were poorly prepared. I'm talking about periods of bliss interspersed with emotional suffocation—all with the same person.

The death of a spouse is often emotionally devastating. Losing a husband to suicide left me in one of the deepest wilderness seasons of my life. As the days and weeks passed, in my mind there were incessant questions as well as physical and emotional exhaustion in my soul and spirit. Teary grief engulfed me as I sorted through all of Lance's documents and personal possessions. I came to realize that if I didn't deal with my grief, the pain and heartache would consume me. Time helped, as well as reaching out for professional counsel, and love and support from professionals, friends, and family. Eventually the grief lessened and even totally dissipated.

The loss of any person close to us, no matter what the reason, results in a whole mess of emotions: shock, guilt, anger, disappointment, denial, or even relief. To one person the loss of a loved one may cause deep and aching grief. To the caregiver, a sense of relief may emerge if they are now relieved of arduous responsibilities of feeding, bathing, and clothing the recently deceased. And there may be a combination of those feelings. Again, it is important to understand and accept our feelings, and then decide what to do with all those feelings.

Identifying your feelings leads to illumination and understanding.

Grief is a natural emotional response to loss. Back in the 1960s Swiss-American psychiatrist Elisabeth Kübler-Ross studied near-death experiences and came up with a theory identifying the five stages of grief. According to the Kübler-Ross model, the five emotional states of terminally ill patients are denial, anger, bargaining, depression, and acceptance.

This may apply for some, but each of us walks through loss and grief differently. Obviously we have to process grief in order to navigate through it, and processing is no five-step pathway. It might be days or weeks of a tough time. Be patient with yourself, and use the *Trusted Tools* in this book to help you avoid months and years of dealing with unresolved grief.

My past and present experiences influence the way I respond to grief. I watched others and learned from them. While that helped, I had little understanding on how to work through my own mental, emotional, and physical losses until I acquired the right tools I'm sharing with you here.

Material Loss

Earthquakes, fires, floods, and tsunamis cause people to lose their homes and a lifetime of irreplaceable possessions. Losing material possessions—money, homes, automobiles, inheritances, a cell phone—can be a very emotional experience. Navigating this extreme devastation may require the help of a professional. And a key Trusted Tool is turning to the One who is always there.

During a one-on-one conversation with an acquaintance, I learned that twenty years prior his family's home was decimated by fire caused by his neighbor's fireworks. His face wrinkled with grief as he spoke about the loss of everything.

"To this day the smell of smoke sets me off," he told me.

Tragedies in life are as real as are the emotions they evoke.

Navigate your material loss wilderness by asking friends, family, professionals, and God to come alongside you for support.

Financial Loss

Nearly every day we keep an eye on our cash flow. When in college, we have tuition. When we have a job, we receive a paycheck and pay bills. When we retire, we live on a specified income. Along our financial journey if we experience a decrease in income, how are we not disappointed?

I've had seasons of both financial abundance and also financial lack. During a time when I had plenty of money, the responsibility of sowing (charitable giving) and investing was super serious to me. I diligently sought out professional financial counsel, personal and spiritual counsel, and prayed a lot about how and where to invest and give. With my personal perspective that everything we have belongs to the One who created it—to God—I steward (manage) my stuff and make the best decisions I can.

When I had financial abundance, I invested in growing businesses, which promised excellent returns within one or two years. I honestly believed this to be the best use of a portion of the money. After many years there was no monetary return on any of the investments. Nada. Zilch. How did that happen?

Several people with whom I invested, deceived me—literally stole from me. That's not a judgment; that's a fact.

Suddenly my monthly income was not enough to pay my expenses. Had I invested differently I would not have been in that situation. Was it a mistake?

It's not a mistake if you learn from it.

I had to reset my compass in order to properly navigate my financial wilderness of unfortunate investments. The reset started by forgiving myself and letting go! I made the best decisions I could at the time, and while the financial wilderness was really difficult, I learned from it. I couldn't remain stuck in the mucky negative emotions surrounding those decisions.

Adding to my pain, a close friend accused me of not giving enough to their personal charity. Though I had already contributed a lot, they said I should do more. Ouch! I felt unfairly judged and very hurt.

There were others who judged me for the car I drove. What they didn't know was I received a friend and family discount. Also, due to a back problem I had to drive a smooth riding, larger vehicle. When the lease on that vehicle expired and I went to lease a new one, the dealer didn't even look at my income; they just assumed I could pay. Had they looked at my income, I wouldn't have qualified for a good bicycle! I learned to be careful of judging; there may be quite a story beyond what you see on the surface.

What did I do in the midst of my financial loss? First, I had to work through my tumultuous emotions which wasn't easy. Next, I pondered whether or not I should speak to the individuals involved. In some cases I could, and in other instances I couldn't. Once again, I had to forgive. Actually... I *chose* to forgive.

I knew I had to move on and this Trusted Tool helped me deal with financial loss:

"If [the devil's] caught, he has to pay back what he stole sevenfold; his punishment and fine will cost him greatly." (Proverbs 6:31 TPT)

In light of the above verse I asked God to deal with the losses. The lessons from this financial wilderness were: forgive myself and others, trust in a bigger plan than what I could see, and trust God to take care of all my needs.

During times of great loss, my mother always said...

"I just keep looking at what I still have."

Change

All sorts of life changes can bring on mental, emotional, and physical tumult. Let's start by looking at the people in our lives.

People

A new baby in a home brings lots of joy, and the little darling also totally flips the way the family functions.

When my son was born, my hormones were out of whack, and my words and behaviors were a wreck. I freaked out over a red squirrel endlessly clawing away at the roofline right above my bedroom. The critter was interfering with my sleep and preventing me from fully enjoying my precious new baby. I was sleep deprived and a trifle emotional. Well, that's an understatement. My mother and husband were about to call the doctor and ask what to do with me. I wasn't functioning in a way any of us expected. A few days after the squirrel situation was resolved I finally settled down. As a result, everyone else settled down too.

Entering into an exciting new relationship may seem like a dream come true. Our "feel-good" hormones get a boost even making us more productive. Starting a new college course or a new job with double the benefits or getting a raise or the softness of a sister's just-born baby in our arms—all of these experiences can be thrilling. And that's all great. However, even the positive stress known as eustress, if it persists too long, can adversely affect our body. Eustress can cause high levels of cortisol and adrenaline potentially affecting parts of the brain causing high blood pressure and other physical symptoms. "But I want to feel good," you might say. Of course we do, and that's a good thing, in moderation.

The upside of positive stress is when we focus on the good times and have faith, we will eventually feel better. It actually helps us to get through the wilderness. Reflecting on good times also increases our faith that things will improve.

Believe and declare,
"Life will get better!"

Jobs, Careers, and New Living Arrangements

Situational losses occur when we are thrown into unexpected situations. Losing a job for example may require moving back in with parents, having a curfew and chores, or going back on a budget that won't even pay for basic necessities.

At the other end of the spectrum, perhaps a family member needs to move in with you resulting in a loss of privacy and free time. Either scenario may leave us feeling like someone unwound our rope in the harbor and pushed our boat out to sea. Anchor me please!

Loss of Health

Loss of well-being due to illness, disease, physical impairment, surgery, or an accident can be profoundly emotional. I suffered for years with health challenges—bronchitis as a baby; mononucleosis as a teenager; and as an adult MRSA (staph infection) and Lyme disease, mercury and mold toxicity, tumors, cysts, and major surgery. During illnesses, my energy levels were tied to my mental and emotional responses. My perceptions were skewed. When your body tries to be master over all else—it's not good. After one surgical procedure, out-of-control emotionally driven words gushed out of my mouth; I wasn't nice. I got so agitated with everyone, everything, and myself. "I can't even stand myself. I'm going to bed!" I shouted.

My mother was victorious over four lung cancer surgeries and many others. Through it all she always said, "I know I'll get through this." Because of her faith even times of extreme pain, physical immobility, and debilitating illness, didn't get her down. She knew from where her strength came, and it wasn't herself. She knew the scripture well, "The Lord God is my strength" (Habakkuk 3:19 NKJV).

"I know I'll get through this!"

If you have a persistent physical affliction, seek the best information available to determine how to handle it. Your research may include doctors, naturopaths, physical or massage therapy, exercise, chiropractic work, acupuncture, essential oils, nutritional counseling, and internet resources. And remember what mama said, "You can't believe everything you read." Seek, discern, research, and pray for wisdom.

During high school, and for several summers afterward, I was a dental assistant. Later, after graduating from college I worked as a dental hygienist. This was in the olden days, prior to facemasks and gloves being the norm in offices. As the dentist drilled and removed old amalgam fillings (metals and mercury), a powdery grey cloud filled the room. I didn't think too much of it as I was focused keeping patients comfortable. When refilling the amalgam-dispensing device, the occasionally spilled bits of roly-poly mercury on the countertop were humorously elusive as I tried to capture them.

What seemed innocuous at the time, years later caused serious illness. I was diagnosed with acute mercury toxicity. My mercury levels were consistent with industrial toxic exposure. Numb with shock I wanted to blame someone: the dentist, the American Dental Association, anyone! In reality it wasn't anyone's fault—I had a choice. I could focus on how devastated I felt, or I could change my thinking and be grateful for finally having an explanation for my many years of extreme fatigue. After emotional jockeying, I eventually chose gratitude and focused on the upside of the situation.

Accepting the reality of the circumstance I made decisive choices to improve my health. Eliminating the mercury from my body required years of in-office intravenous chelation treatments, at-home chelation, and nutritional supplements. After every treatment I became nauseous and fatigued. It was a tough wilderness while continuing as wife, mother, and volunteer.

I was very grateful to have time in my schedule for the appointments, the financial resources for the treatments, and that my old silver fillings had previously been replaced. Had they not that would have been the first protocol. I maintained faith and hope that all the treatments would work, and eventually I would feel better. I intentionally chose to focus on the positive—a decision and choice in the mind and heart.

Loss of Dreams, Desires or Hope

Dreams and desires are our innermost longings. Sometimes life doesn't work out as we hope or imagine. The dreams and desires of our heart don't come true. The ideal university, the job, the romantic relationship—not there. Maybe marriage and children haven't manifested. We want to be healthy; we want our family to be healthy, but everyone seems to have some sort of illness. When our dreams, desires, and hopes don't come to fruition, disappointment and discouragement try to creep in. You can and will get through this wilderness. Jump to Chapter 8 for solutions.

One of the deepest wilderness seasons is loss of hope, a primary contributing factor to suicide. As you read in Chapter 1, I experienced this firsthand. When Lance took his own life, the questions endlessly raced through my mind. "Why? Was he in heaven? What in the world could cause him to want to die rather than live? What happens now for me and my son?"

For years, I wrestled with these questions until a tremendous blessing brought me understanding. One of his Veterans Administration reports identified he had PTSD, and the people from the healing room shared further information. Now a few more pieces to Lance's puzzle were coming together. But what if one doesn't ever get information leading to understanding? It is often beyond our comprehension for someone to take their own life. We are left hanging, never knowing the thought processes which led them into hopelessness and despair. So then what?

First, if you know someone who committed suicide, I implore you, don't blame yourself. It's rather far-fetched that it would be your fault. Unfortunately there is little you or anyone else could have done to change their mind, especially when you don't see any signs.

There is a hope that never fails.

If your friends, family, or coworkers talk of lacking a purpose or feeling hopeless, isolated, or depressed, listen carefully! Someone considering suicide sometimes gives subtle hints. If you pick up on this, be bold and ask. Your questions might save a life. A friend saw that his daughter was depressed and despondent; he was worried she might do something drastic. He encouraged her to get involved with a positive, uplifting group of individuals, and she did. The discouragement lifted, and she is now happier, feels connected and dad is no longer concerned.

Without hope we are enroute to becoming a directionless wilderness wanderer. With hope, vision, and purpose we become a steady traveler moving with intentionality in a guided direction. From where do we get that guided direction? From knowing our identity as children of a heavenly Father. More on that later.

Life Change and Identity

Major life changes *seem* (the operative word here is seem) to influence our identity. You attend college or school, and you are a *student*. You get married and you're a *husband* or a *wife*. You have a baby, and you're a *parent*. A relationship ends, and you're *single*. You lose a spouse, and you're a *widow* or *widower*. You write a book and you're an *author*.

These circumstantial life changes might feel like they change who we are, but who we are is not defined by our circumstances, our career, or our lifestyle. Circumstances identify our role in the moment. When we know our true identity, for what we are created, and our purpose in life, our identity is established on a solid foundation. (Identity is unpacked in Chapter 8.)

Perception vs Reality of Loss

There are actual losses and then there are perceived losses. Perceived losses are real in your mind but are based upon what you *think* has happened without proof that such has occurred. Nonetheless, perceived losses can trigger all the same emotions as actual losses. Whether one or the other, both feel stressful!

For example, the loss of a job may cause lowered self-esteem. A mother who feels lonely because the children don't call or text much may think her bond with them has lessened. A boy who feels unloved or unaffirmed by his father may feel a loss of self-esteem or self-worth. A lack of parental love can lead a child to feelings of unworthiness and rejection and result in anger. All of these situations feel like genuine losses, but are they real?

We have thousands of thoughts in a day. To function at our peak we must carefully consider the perceptions versus realities of our thoughts. As mentioned in Chapter 2, our emotional responses are the result of how we perceive and therefore how we think about a situation. Realistic perceptions and thoughts result in emotions and responses consistent with the situation. Are your thoughts based on a reality? Let's have frequent reality checks—I know I need them.

Situations create perceptions which create thoughts which create emotions which create responses.

Stress

Navigating change by directing and/or redirecting our thoughts leads to less stress. In our minds we create perceptions about situations and circumstances. We have thoughts based on truth or non-truths. These thoughts then create emotions and responses.

What feels stressful to you right now?

What is your perception of the stress in that situation?

Are your thoughts based on a tangible or intangible reality?

Our perceptions are *our* reality, but is your perception

lined up with the *actual* reality of the situation?

What are the thoughts created as a result of that perception?

Why does this feel like stress? What feels like pressure?

I had a lot of physical reactions to stress: fatigue, confusion, sleeplessness, you name it. With every stressful thought, a complex mix of hormones and chemicals were released, affecting my emotions, brain, and body. Eventually I understood that the way I was thinking, and my perceptions were leading me into dark places. I had to grab hold of my thoughts and learn how to navigate them. This is an important tool to conquer the stress wilderness.

Stress is pressure we put on ourselves due to our thoughts.

My friend Sophia was super stressed out because she *thought* her business associate, Abigail, didn't do what she asked her to do.

"I had asked Abigail to call Connor and ask for the money up front," Sophia told me. "And I *just know* she didn't!" Sophia was upset because she *thought* Abigail didn't ask Connor for the money.

"Did Abigail *tell* you she didn't ask for the money up front?" I asked.

"Well, no, but I could tell by the way she was talking."

I said, "You can't assume she did or didn't ask for the money until you specifically ask her if she did."

Remember the perception vs reality discussion? Turns out she created a scenario in her head possibly not matching up with reality.

Work Through It or Work to Get Out

Some wilderness seasons last a few minutes, others last a few years. Does it matter how long you stay in the wilderness? Maybe. Some people choose to stay in a wilderness because they've become comfortable there. It becomes the place where they know how to function: the zone they know. But, staying in the zone they know for too long may not be the best zone to grow.

When you muster up the courage to deal with your emotions and you work to move out of a wilderness cycle, you become a conqueror. From my own experiences, I assure you it's worth every minute of intentional effort to get out of the wilderness and also to learn and grow while you're there. So, go to it and conquer that wilderness!

Wonderful transitions are available in you, for you, and through you during the wilderness. A few keys I learned while navigating the wilderness:

~ Accept the situation in your head (unless abuse is involved).

~ Understand how the situation affects your emotions.

~ Increase your understanding of how to deal with those emotions.

~ Learn to readjust and/or redirect your focus and thinking.

~ Explore whether you, or someone else, is able to change the situation.

~ Look for what could be helpful in the situation.

~ Expect to get through it and know you'll be okay.

Consistently using these keys, I learned to get through even the toughest times with less anxiety, less stress, and less fear. In those dark times, I began to have moments when divine inspiration, illumination, and realization allowed me to see, feel, and experience an increase of faith, hope, and peace.

Be encouraged!
Your tools are here.

TOOLBOX

◻ Reflect on losses you've experienced that are causing you grief now, or caused you grief in the past. If painful memories come up and it feels uncomfortable, remember the intention is to acknowledge grief, to understand if you've worked through it, and to be sure you've come out of it. If you feel grief is hanging on and you can't get over it, consider speaking with a professional. Resources are at the end of the book.

◻ Write out your dreams, visions, desires, and hopes. Act as though there is no limitation of time or resources. How can you actively work toward any of these?

◻ Did you ever seem to lose something, which led to undesirable feelings then later realize those feelings didn't line up with the perceived loss? Describe the scenario.

◻ What feels stressful or like a pressure to you right now? What are your perceptions and your thoughts about that situation?

◻   How can you change your perception? How
    can you change the way you think about the
    situation?

◻   Consider a wilderness season you went
    through. What did you experience during
    that time? Now that you have the tools, how
    will you navigate future wilderness seasons
    differently?

CHAPTER 5

How Do I Know What I Don't Know?

Divine Design

Consider this a possibility—you are divinely designed and there's a plan for your life. Given we are spiritual beings, entertain the idea that the Divine (God) communicates with you about the plan for your life and wants to guide and encourage you throughout the process. In the same way as your body is designed to heal itself, your spirit is also designed to grow, develop, and be interconnected to the Divine One.

Think of a time when you had a strong gut feeling about something. Was it a physical feeling, a sort of tension in your body? Did you have a flash of a picture in your mind or an unexpected emotion? Did you hear or imagine you heard a word or words? Did you follow your gut instinct or not? What was the result? Do you use your gut feelings to make decisions? Did you consider that it might be the Divine One communicating with you through the power of Holy Spirit?

Discernment

The tension in your body, the flash of a picture in your mind, an unexpected little voice in your head, your hair standing on end, or a sudden emotion—these sensations may be developed into spiritual discernment, which represents an inner knowing which goes beyond intellectual understanding. By receiving God (who is Spirit) in your heart and in *your* spirit, you then receive Holy Spirit who helps you make decisions and guides your journey through those gut feelings, those pictures, sounds, words, and emotions. Spiritual discernment is activated through contemplation, reflection, prayer, and meditation (listening).

Discernment provides you with insight and good judgment. During those wilderness days or seasons, discernment will help you know if you should chill and stay for a while, what to do while you're in that experience and how and when to move ahead and get out of it.

Each wilderness is unique. Applying the insights and tools you've already learned plus implementing discernment will help you through tough times.

Discernment is key for navigating
tough times and all of life!

TOOLBOX

☐ Think of a time when you had a gut feeling or strong sensation that actually became a reality. Was it a physical feeling, a tension in your body or maybe something else? Describe whether a picture flashed through your mind, or an unexpected emotion gave you chills.

☐ Did you ping someone at the exact same time they were pinging you? Why do you think that happens? Describe a time when you sensed something and then it happened.

☐ Think of a time when you followed your gut instinct—when you made a decision after a lot of thought and then "just knew" it was the right one. What was the result?

☐ Our upbringing, experiences, and circumstances influence what we choose to believe. How do any or all of them affect your spirituality and your discernment?

☐ What steps would you like to take to increase your discernment?

☐ Would you like to communicate with a higher being to increase your discernment? What would that look like? (Jump to Chapter 7 for a few pointers.)

CHAPTER 6

What's Up With The Wait?

You've been waiting and waiting in the wilderness and you just want out. The emotional frenzy from dealing with difficulties and drama just plain stinks! That "Don't Worry, Be Happy" song makes your hair stand on end. It seems impossible. You're not happy. You're anxious and disappointed with the wait.

What if during those tough times there were useful guides to help you through and eventually lead you back to the light of your spirit? And what if, during that journey, you were molded and shaped into a better form of yourself?

 **Trusted Tool**

You might be in the wilderness for a reason.

Keeping your eyes, ears, and heart open to all possibilities enhances the wilderness experience. "Keep your thoughts continually fixed on all that is authentic and real, honorable and admirable, beautiful and respectful, pure and holy, merciful and kind. And fasten your thoughts on every glorious work of God, praising him always" (Philippians 4:8 TPT)

We've extensively explored our thinking. So now, let's use the wisdom from the above biblical words to give us tools and direction on HOW to think differently. Pretty cool.

God Wants to Do What in Me?

With an open heart I share my personal tough times to give you hope. I've experienced hardships: abuse, divorce, loss of a baby, extreme health issues, and suicide. Through all of these, my go-to guide was and is the Word of God—the Bible. I believe the words are true. Reading and believing the word of God is *the* reason I'm no longer in professional counseling, and at the same time, I frequently counsel with close friends and family.

Due to Lance's addiction and anger issues, at times my marriage was a desolate wilderness. And because I wasn't healed from my own junk, I didn't have the proper tools to help the relationship. Lance was a reservist in the US Army and a financial planner. He was highly intelligent, sought excellence, and obtained several advanced-level financial planning certifications. Twice activated for Operation Enduring Freedom, he served two tours in Afghanistan. During his second deployment he was awarded a Bronze Star Medal.

He presented himself to the world as happy, competent, and caring, which part of him was. The other parts could be entirely different. The first time I knew something wasn't quite right happened when we were watching a movie and he fell asleep. Suddenly, he started yelling and screaming in terror. What was going on? I was undone! When he settled down, he explained it was just a bad dream. At the time I didn't know him very well, and it was only after we were married that the bad dreams proved to be a consistent pattern.

Lance enjoyed his first tour in Afghanistan as he assisted the locals in rebuilding roads, schools, and hospitals. He particularly loved providing aid and assistance at an orphanage. The second deployment was dramatically different. After returning he often referred to the extreme challenges and personality dynamics with individuals on the base. As he spoke about it the pain and trauma in his voice was evident; I sensed he felt verbally abused. Upon his return his anger, moodiness, and self-imposed isolation became excessive.

Our communication was horrible including long periods without any conversation at all. Lance would withdraw for days and even weeks at a time, leaving our marriage in an emotionally isolated wilderness. Our life together felt like an empty, lifeless tomb.

Lance spiraled into irrational tirades directed at me. My knee-jerk reaction was to defend myself from his false accusations. Thankfully he didn't do this in front of my son. I tried to reason with him about the lies he believed to be true and to speak the truth about how I saw each situation. It didn't work. I felt frustrated, miserable, hurt, and disappointed. It was all very confusing. How could this man be so loving, kind, and generous yet also be irrational, angry, and withdrawn? I started seeing a counselor with whom Lance had previously visited hoping he would eventually join us. He did. But several minutes into our first and only session he stood up and yelled, "It's always about me! I'm not listening to this!" and stormed out of the office. Later I realized his reaction was a smoke screen to hide the pornography addiction.

At that time, post-traumatic stress disorder (PTSD) was not widely acknowledged. I tried to discuss depression and PTSD symptoms; he refused the conversations. At times his sharp words cut my soul. Life was a traumatic and emotional roller-coaster. If we tried to discuss our issues, he became defensive, and the conversation went nowhere. It is so true that what we speak reflects what is in our hearts. Lance's heart was deeply wounded.

My illuminating moment in conquering this wilderness came with the wise words of two friends.

"Lana, this isn't about Lance. This is about what God wants to do in you." Mic drop!

"What?" I defensively fired back. "But he's the one who—"

Blah, blah, blah. They stopped me. "This isn't about Lance. What does God want to do through *you* in all this?"

That was tough to hear. In my mind Lance was the one with the issues. At the same time, as I was trying to defend myself I was contributing to the contention. I needed to change. I needed to make a choice. The choice in my mind became an action of my will. I decided to listen to the counsel of my dear friends and ditch the mindset that this was all about him.

It wasn't an overnight fix. It took weeks to mentally and emotionally process the advice and to start taking personal responsibility for changing myself. I didn't know what that looked like. It seemed easier said than done. Eventually I asked God, "What do you want to do in me? How do you want to change me? What do you want me to do and to be in this marriage?"

I was asking God, but how would I know for certain I was hearing from Him? That's where discernment comes in. I turned to His Word to see what it said about wives and husbands. This choice was a conquering moment in my life. Here is what I found:

> Always give thanks to Father God for every person
> he brings into your life in the name of our Lord
> Jesus Christ. And out of your reverence for Christ
> be supportive of each other in love. For wives, this
> means being devoted to your husbands like you
> are tenderly devoted to our Lord, for the husband
> provides leadership for the wife, just as Christ
> provides leadership for his church, as the Savior and
> Reviver of the body. In the same way the church is
> devoted to Christ, let the wives be devoted to their
> husbands in everything. And to the husbands, you
> are to demonstrate love for your wives with the same
> tender devotion that Christ demonstrated to us, his
> bride. (Ephesians 5:20–25 TPT)

The Lesson

Heaven, help me! How was I going to be supportive and devoted when I was distraught, overwhelmed, and feeling like it was all his fault? I had to take a real, raw look at myself to find out why I was reacting the way I was. I needed professional help and ran after it. Several Christian counselors helped me work through my lifetime of programming, and I began to understand how it was affecting me. Old wounds and hurts needed to be identified, forgiven, and released.

Eventually, I stopped arguing with Lance. As much as it went against my old self, I made every effort to speak gently, and if I could not control my emotions, I removed myself from the situation. When an argument was about to blow up, I left the house for a few hours to settle down. I would drive to a parking lot and call a friend or go visit one for support and prayer. I wanted to respond calmly from my spirit—a place I could go only with the help of Holy Spirit—and not react from my emotions.

"Respond gently when you are confronted, and you'll defuse the rage of another. Responding with sharp, cutting words will only make it worse." (Proverbs 15:1 TPT)

I learned I shouldn't try to defend myself when he was, in my opinion, irrational. I had to give it up. This was a monumental mind-set shift. In the past, when feeling verbally attacked, I verbally defended myself; it was instinctive. Pretty soon, I knew fighting back or trying to rationalize the situation wasn't going to help. I realized responding from my spirit and not reacting out of my emotions couldn't be accomplished on my own. In the middle of a hot mess argument, I prayed under my breath, asking God to help me—asking Holy Spirit to take my emotions, to keep my mouth shut, to put kind words in my mouth, and to help me be respectful. It worked.

Eventually, when Lance got hot and bothered, I was able to remain relatively cool and calm. *Relatively* is the key word here. I vividly remember the day he was torqued about finances and started yelling at me. Through the tears and in a calm voice I said, "What would you like to do? Do you want me to pay the bills? Do you want to pay the bills? Tell me and I'll do whatever you want." He couldn't answer.

For me not to yell and argue back in that emotionally charged exchange was a breakthrough moment. Later, when I understood the extent of Lance's PTSD, I was sorry I didn't learn to get a grip on my emotions sooner (this is where self-forgiveness comes in) and at the same time grateful I had learned to respond more calmly from my spirit rather than reacting out of my emotions. I had learned yet another lesson about the wilderness experience: to get a grip on my emotions and my tongue when I'm upset.

I learned a profound life-lesson. Conflict is not pointing fingers at another person for what they are saying or doing. When conflict arises in a relationship, it presents an opportunity to explore how we can respond differently than our old self. We can learn, we can grow, and we can head in a new direction. And that direction points us out of the wilderness.

And truthfully, to this day I avoid conflict. I don't like it, but each time conflict happens around me, I sit back, assess the situation, take a deep breath, and choose how I will respond.

Patient Endurance

In Chapter 3 we saw how our past wounds, hurts, and thinking affects communication. Any or all of these may cause delays in coming out of the wilderness. Consider a refresher on that chapter and think about how your old self might be in the way of moving forward into your authentic self.

Times of trouble and pressure lead us to patient endurance. Right?! Okay, a little sarcasm. How in the world are we patient during tough times when we feel crummy and under pressure? Let's differentiate between our emotions and our spirit. Emotions are what we feel, while joy for example, known as a fruit of the spirit, is more than an emotion. It is, well, a spiritual thing. We can be emotionally upset and disappointed, while at the same time have spiritual joy. Say what?

As I wandered through my own wilderness seasons, I became aware of how my emotions and thoughts tried to trip me up. I'm now attentive to this dynamic every day. When I get upset or anxious, I press into listening to my internal dialogue. Remember that self-talk thing? When I start thinking negatively, I get anxious and have to press the pause button and ask myself, "Why are you thinking that way? What is pushing your buttons and causing anxiety?" With this discovery and understanding, I now intentionally shift my thoughts to what is positive, opening my spirit to joy, and redirecting my thoughts to what is true.

Recognizing what makes us feel pressured and anxious are opportunities to:

~ Develop patient endurance,
~ Refine our character,
~ Increase hope because we know it's temporary, and
~ Discover and know the endless love of God.

A friend asked how I was doing, and I told her I was in the wilderness. My tone of voice prompted her words of wisdom: "The Lord must want to do something in you and through you. Receive it." Though I knew her words were true, it wasn't what I wanted to hear. I was annoyed with the thought of having to wait while the Lord worked on me. At the same time I felt convicted by her words and knew she was right; I needed to change my attitude.

Many of us are instant gratification junkies. Cell phones, computers, and voice-command devices surround us. With a few clicks or a shout, the world is at our beck and call. Our lives are full; we have tons of responsibilities and demands. We want what we want, and we want it now—so patience doesn't come naturally.

Patience is twofold: emotional and mental. We can feel impatient (emotionally) waiting in a long line at the grocery store or we can choose to be patient (mentally) while we wait. No way?! Yes way. Choosing patience requires first recognizing we feel impatient and then shifting our thinking to mentally accept standing in that line and waiting. Once we recognize the emotional side of impatience., then we can shift to our mental side of it, hopefully easing into calmly waiting in line. Impatience can lead to increase in blood pressure, irritability and even anger. Once we identify the *feeling* of impatience, we can choose to redirect our thoughts. Redirecting and refocusing our thoughts toward something positive helps us conquer our emotions and become patient without the anxiety.

Standing in that line for extended periods of time may evoke many emotions, but what if at that moment we are conscious of our spiritual connection to God? That time in line could bring joy to our soul and spirit!

I live in Michigan where construction is pretty much everywhere year-round. One morning I planned the precise time to leave for an appointment, adding in a few extra minutes. Driving toward a major intersection, there they were, the menacing orange barrels. Traffic became stop and go. Drivers began shifting lanes, zooming by me, and cutting in front of others. Who do they think they are, speeding up and cutting in front of all of us who have been waiting so long? You know the ones. And then we were at a standstill and there came the thoughts. "I'm going to be late. My doctor won't be happy. I'll have to reschedule the appointment." Road rage check. Anxiety under stress reared its ugly head as I sat going nowhere. Our responses and reactions are mental and emotional. Which comes first? Hard to say. Let's start with the emotions.

In my construction story I felt impatient, anxious, and irritated at the drivers cutting in line. My pulse and blood pressure increased. Those physical responses were because I was concerned about being late and missing the appointment. And I was ticked off at the drivers cutting in front of everyone. So what did I do with those feelings? I paused and became aware of my thoughts.

I was stressing *myself* out. I couldn't do anything about the drivers speeding around and cutting in line. I needed to give it up. As for being late for the appointment, I had no control over it since the traffic would move when it could. I redirected my thoughts this way: What happens, happens. I have no control over this construction or those other drivers. If I have to reschedule the meeting, I will reschedule. Hey, maybe the doctor will be running behind schedule, and it will all work out. Take a few deep breaths. Relax.

Redirecting + Refocusing = Less Stress

During wilderness seasons, instead of pushing up against and resisting our circumstances, emotions can shift when we choose to be more patient in our heads (our thinking). Again, that doesn't mean we tolerate abusive or harmful situations. Those situations may require professional intervention which is encouraged.

As for being more patient, the real starting place is to be patient with ourselves. When *feeling* impatient, it is possible to make a conscious decision to *be* patient. At times we think, "If I can just control these circumstances, they will change." Trying to overtly control the things we can't change is useless, and we just end up feeling dissatisfied and disappointed. This doesn't mean we sit back and do nothing. When we give up trying to control the circumstances we can't change, we become less frustrated and then we can proceed to work through the situation.

Sometimes we can try and try and try and still can't get no satisfaction. Sounds like the Rolling Stones. Patient endurance develops when we embrace and accept the things we can't change. This is another key to conquering the wilderness—knowing what we can and cannot change by looking at the circumstances from many perspectives and perhaps asking trusted friends or professionals for their input.

Character Chiseling

Our circumstances are a result of (1) our own choices and decisions, (2) someone else's choices and decisions, or (3) what we perceive to be someone else's choices and decisions. Whichever scenario applies, when we are open to it a wilderness experience has purpose. It may even serve to refine our character.

Say what? What purpose is there in feeling frustrated? In feeling lonely? In feeling grief? In a divorce? Why did my brother have to die so young? Why did we lose our child? Why did I have all that illness? These are valid and excellent questions, and oftentimes there aren't great answers. Sorry to say, but some of the *"whys"* in life will remain a mystery. This doesn't mean we give up and stop seeking insight and understanding. Perhaps we will come across tangible explanations and reasons thereby helping us move toward acceptance.

Discerning when to keep asking and when to stop asking requires wisdom.

Getting stuck on the proverbial hamster wheel and continuing to pursue why something happened could result in continued disappointment and discouragement. So what do we do with all these questions and emotions? How do we make peace with the *whys*? One way is deciding to accept the situation even with the unanswered questions.

Part of refining our character is accepting that we may never know or have answers to some of our most painful and challenging questions. A key to refining my character turned when I intentionally brought my emotions to the Comforter. Jesus said, "And I will pray the Father, and he shall give you another Comforter, that he may abide with you forever" (John 14:16 KJV).

Jesus was talking about Holy Spirit and here is a personal example.

In a seven-month period, my husband, stepbrother, and brother died. My family and I were devastated. While grieving, I dealt with my husband's will and related affairs, and then was asked to take on the responsibility of my brother's legal affairs. I spent months on the phone with attorneys, realtors, hospitals, the Department of Veterans Affairs, and businesses. I had court dates and piles of paperwork. I was dragging emotionally, physically, and mentally.

It seemed like every day I was telling a close friend, "I'm so overwhelmed." He gently pointed out that the words we speak are powerful and create our reality. Thanks to the wisdom of my friend, I realized if I kept thinking and saying how overwhelmed I was I *would* continue being overwhelmed. I couldn't deny how I felt, so what could I do? I prayed. I asked God to help me bring this emotion to Him.

I stopped saying "overwhelmed" out loud and replaced it with, "I can do all things through Christ who strengthens me." Did it miraculously take away those feelings? Not quite. In time, though, as I continued to express out loud and in my head, "I can do this," the stress and pressure lessened.

Why character refinement? Because we're not perfect. Loud laugh! I don't know about you, but I want to be a better listener, a better parent, and a better friend. I want to be more like God wants me to be and I realize that such a transition will only come through my relationship with Him.

Anyone remember those WWJD bracelets? *What Would Jesus Do?* Now there's the One who is perfect. What does it look like to have more of His character? We may not fully understand all of who He is, but we can know Him through what He says and does.

"Keep your thoughts continually fixed on all that is authentic and real, honorable and admirable, beautiful and respectful, pure and holy, merciful and kind" (Philippians 4:8 TPT).

One more time—the importance of our thinking. During tough times emotions are a zippy roller-coaster. The more tumultuous the emotions, the more tumultuous our lives. What if we move away from roller-coaster emotions to merry-go-round emotions: smooth, calm, and steady? Can we be calm when all heck is breaking loose? For me, there was one way. I had to search out what good I could find in any situation to keep myself from crumbling.

> You will keep him in perfect peace, whose mind is
> stayed on You, because he trusts in You.
> (Isaiah 26:3 NKJV)

One year during horrific wildfires in California, the driver of a bus carrying schoolchildren feverishly tried to avoid the flames lapping at the road. After making it through successfully, one of the children was asked what she did during this crisis. She said, "I went to my happy place." Calm and steady is possible, during even extreme wilderness times, by focusing on our happy places, the good around us, and especially on the love of God.

How we perceive, think about, and therefore respond to our circumstances is a learned process. For seventeen years I unknowingly lived in a home with a basement contaminated by toxin-producing mold. The invisible poisonous gases (called tricothecene mycotoxins) permeated my entire condo. According to the Center for Disease Control and Prevention these toxins can cause systemic symptoms including weakness, ataxia, hypotension, and death.

After inspecting the basement for the first time, the mold remediation specialist said, "Let's get you out of here!" I couldn't believe it! When we got upstairs, waves of dizziness splashed through my head. The specialist and the accompanying doctor (a mold expert) explained that what I perceived to simply be beams made of grey-colored wood, were actually grey colonies of mold producing deadly toxins that were poisoning me.

Every single item, whether a button or a key, a dresser or a sofa, had to be treated or tossed in the trash. Every day for two weeks, I covered every inch of my body—head covering, facemask, gloves, and protective clothing—as I entered the toxic basement to sort through a lifetime of personal possessions, many of which were not replaceable. I cried at least once a day. I was physically sick and emotionally exhausted. I couldn't ask anyone to help me. Who do you ask to help clean up your toxic house?

Through the tears I continuously prayed and cried out, "God, help me! This is just too much. I'm exhausted and I'm sick!"

The task was daunting, and at the same time I was grateful to finally have an answer to the brain fog and chronic fatigue. The mycotoxin (the invisible toxins produced by certain molds) exposure had greatly weakened my immune system, which likely contributed to me having MRSA (Methicillin-resistant Staphylococcus aureus) and Lyme disease. I couldn't deny my feelings, or diagnoses, while at the same time, I felt some comfort, knowing every day was a step toward a healthier home and my physical healing. Gratitude was mixed with anguish. I was grateful the source of illness had been discovered, and I was in anguish at the magnitude of the cleanup. And then God showed up and the job got completed.

When I got to the point of frantic frustration and simply needed a pair of scissors, there they were, right next to me. When I needed another garbage bag, I turned, and one was right there. Forty large garbage bags bursting with possessions went to the curb. When I was overcome with sadness at throwing away cherished family heirlooms, I was able to do it, knowing my life literally depended on it.

"Call to Me, and I will answer you."
(Jeremiah 33:3 NKJV)

I needed God. I kept looking for God. When I did, I began to see His provision. I prayed for strength and I continued to receive it. Did God "magically" put scissors and garbage bags at my side when I needed them? No. He's not a magician, but I called to Him and that's when I felt like He answered. I was able to see Him in many little things. That's when I knew I wasn't alone.

By shifting my focus to Him and the ultimate goal (an environmentally safe home), I was able to shift my thinking from what I was losing to what I was gaining. To keep from getting depressed at letting go of cherished items, I focused on what I still had. Focusing on Him, calling out to Him, and reaching out to my friends and family helped me conquer that intense wilderness.

Initially my thoughts were negative, "This is so overwhelming, I hate this! I can't believe I have to throw away my grandmother's handmade dolls and her paintings." My mind-set and emotions shifted when I started thinking, "Thank goodness the mold was discovered; thank goodness I have a doctor who knows how to treat me; thank goodness for the specialist who uses non-toxic remediation methods." This is how I found peace and hope during a terribly tough time.

Reflecting back, I realize the mold experience was not just about the destination (getting the job done) but also about the journey. By travelling that wilderness journey I learned to trust God more by:

~ Recognizing how I felt,

~ Sharing all my feelings with Him (He saw every tear),

~ Looking for Him,

~ Asking Him to be with me and help me, and

~ Believing He was with me.

Grateful

A dear friend gave me a hot pink leather journal titled, "Start each day with a grateful heart." Just looking at that cheerful journal and title makes me feel grateful. When a cloud of wilderness worry drifts my way, I take out that pink journal, my pink pen, and I write and write and write about anything and everything for which I am grateful. Sometimes it's as simple as heat in my home, warm blankets, or good coffee (that's in the journal often). Sometimes I write about gratitude for bigger things. Though my desire for a dream house had not yet happened, I focused on being grateful for the condo I did have. I chose my thinking. I chose my focus. Making these choices helped keep out negative emotions. And to this day when the negative thoughts and emotions try to creep in I say, "Back off!"

"Eyes that focus on what is beautiful bring joy to the heart." (Proverbs 15:30 TPT)

Does it Have to Hurt?

Why do we have to go through tough times? If God loves us, why does He let so much horrible stuff happen in our lives and in the world? And why do we sometimes stay in our wilderness for so long? When we are asking, we are seeking, and that's good. Exploring why we are where we are and why we are experiencing pain and tough times, brings insight and helps us develop strategies for growth as we move into our next season.

Why painful times? The answers are many and there isn't a simple one, but here are a few ideas to consider. Tough times:

~ Can cultivate empathy and compassion in us which can be extended to others,

~ Help us to reevaluate our priorities and values,

~ Bring us to a place of peace as we learn to seek contentment,

~ Help us discover courage to keep going, and

~ Give us resilience and strength.

Remember that discernment thing? Here is where it comes into play. We learn to discern whether we are to stay in the wilderness for a season or take strategic action to get out. Each journey is an opportunity to activate faith, and gain the hope and belief that your wilderness will end.

Ready to conquer your wilderness?

Using discernment to determine
if you can change a situation ask
yourself, Can I change it?
If you can't change it, ask yourself,
What do I do while I wait?
If you can change it, ask yourself,
What needs to happen next?

If your situation is one that cannot be changed, or you're choosing to remain in that place, then discover how you can become content where you are.

Contentment

Patience and contentment are linked. The apostle Paul, one of Jesus' close followers, was considered to be a troublemaker and got locked up in prison for talking about Jesus. During his prison time he said, "I have learned to be content whatever the circumstances. I know what it is to be in need, and I know what it is to have plenty. I have learned the secret of being content in any and every situation, whether well fed or hungry, whether living in plenty or in want. I can do everything through Him who gives me strength." (Philippians 4:11–13 NIV).

What is the "secret?" This kind of patience and contentment is spiritual—from God rather than emotional (from our feelings) or intellectual (from our thinking).

What's the "secret sauce?" For me, whenever I get anxious, feel life is stagnant, and want to move ahead but need to be patient, I tell myself, "If Paul could be content in a prison, surely I can be content where I am!" Contentment becomes a mindset through one's choice. It comes from:

~ Focusing on and appreciating what we have.
~ Not focusing on what we don't have or what is missing.
~ Letting go of comparisons.
~ Keeping an attitude of gratitude by filling our mind with encouraging and uplifting readings, music, movies, and stories.

~ Being grateful.
~ Having realistic expectations.
~ Taking care of yourself; tending to your own health, mind, will and emotions.

Be content with what you have, because God has said, "Never will I leave you; never will I forsake you." (Hebrews 13:5 NIV)

TOOLBOX

◻ Describe a situation where you waited a long time for something and later realized the wait was beneficial or served a purpose.

◻ What lesson(s) did you learn while waiting?

◻ Is there something in your past, your old self, that is keeping you from moving forward? Causing a delay?

◻ What tools can you implement to become more patient and content?

◻ What is there in your life for which you can be thankful?

CHAPTER 7

WHO IS HE?

Whether you know Him or not, God is close—waiting to help you conquer the wilderness. I got through the wilderness by activating my faith in Him. His love is all encompassing and He is omnipotent—which means all powerful. So who is this God?

Who is God?

How can I know or experience a divine being I can't see or have never touched? Good question. This is where a more detailed discussion of our mind, will, soul, and spirit take center stage. I shared stories of how I personally experienced God, so now let's explore how you can do the same.

I Can't See Him

God is spirit. We experience and communicate with Him through our spirit. We use our mind to think and to choose what we believe. We have a will, and we make choices. We have emotions based on thoughts and feelings. We have a soul, which is the mind, will, and emotions all working together. And then we have our spirit, which connects us to God and enables us to communicate with and experience Him—spirit to spirit.

While the concept of God varies across different spiritual and religious beliefs, I (and billions throughout history) have come to rely on the number-one best-selling book in the history of the world, the Holy Bible. Through those Bible stories the essence and character of God is revealed. The Bible contains God-inspired words that were placed into the spirit of man, conveyed by word of mouth, which were then written down. To believe the Bible is 100 percent God's truth is a matter of one's choice and an exercise of faith.

In one simple and yet profound statement, the essence of God is love. His character is love. His being is love. Here's how the Bible describes love:

> Love is large and incredibly patient. Love is gentle
> and consistently kind to all. It refuses to be jealous
> when blessing comes to someone else. Love does
> not brag about one's achievements nor inflate its
> own importance. Love does not traffic in shame and
> disrespect, nor selfishly seek its own honor. Love
> is not easily irritated or quick to take offense. Love
> joyfully celebrates honesty and finds no delight in
> what is wrong. Love is a safe place of shelter for it
> never stops believing the best for others. Love never
> takes failure as defeat for it never gives up.
> (1 Corinthians 13:4–7 TPT)

Take a moment and read those words slowly and out loud. Allow your whole being, mind, will, emotions and spirit to receive the essence of these words.

Another name for God is Lord. Here are just a few of many, many descriptions of God in the Bible. God is:

The eternal Creator
The Lord our sovereign
The Lord our provider
The Lord our banner
The Lord our healer
The Lord our peace
The Lord our righteousness
The Lord our sanctifier
The Lord of hosts
The Lord is present
The Lord most high
The Lord my shepherd
The Lord our maker
The Lord our God
The Lord my God

Creator

When we create anything—a homework assignment, a meal, what we write on social media, a painting, a piece of music, or a smoothie—it begins with a thought constructed and shaped in our imagination.

The first verse in the Bible says, "In the beginning God created the heavens and the earth."

God has an imagination by which He creates, just like we can do. He created everything. He created the heavens and the earth, night and day, the waters, the mountains, well... everything on the planet and in the sky, including you and me. The vastness of our planet, the solar system and the universe, is beyond my comprehension. Is it all random? I think not.

Guess what? We can tap into that same divine creativity and apply it to our lives because "We have the mind of Christ" (1 Corinthians 2:16 NKJV). Our ability to think, process, create, love, problem solve or experience joy, peace, patience, and kindness is all possible because of how God created us.

Heavenly Father & Earthly Father

Some of us grew up with biological fathers who were less than ideal; angry, abusive, liars, cheaters, or absent. The parental figures in our lives with the primary responsibility to nurture, protect, guide, and love us sometimes abandoned their responsibility. A wounded parent or guardian who is not able to love and nurture others leaves those around them emotionally betrayed and confused as to what love is and what love looks like.

As we grow up our views and perceptions of a father are formed by our interactions with the father figure in our lives and from our personal experiences. If the actions of our earthly father are hurtful, the emotional and spiritual wounds of the soul remain until healed. And now for some really good news! Our heavenly Father has no negative attributes. We can't compare our earthly father with our heavenly Father because our heavenly Father is perfect. His character is love, mercy, and grace. "See what kind of love the Father has given to us, that we should be called children of God; and so we are" (1 John 3:1 ESV).

The subject of fathers is massively important, so please pay particular attention to the *Toolbox* at the end of this chapter. If when you process your relationship with your father it starts feeling painful, reach out to a friend, family member, minister, pastor, or professional to guide you along the way. On the other hand, if your father was kind, loving, and caring then it may be easier to embrace the concept of the love of your heavenly Father. In either case God's love is beyond what my finite brain is able to grasp. Here's an example of what God's love can do.

I grew up with a father who at times was verbally, and sometimes physically abusive. All the while, he worked diligently to provide for our family. He supported us four children in our activities whether it was cheerleading, baseball, or city projects. Our lives were a roller-coaster ride of ups when he was good and kind and downs when he was angry. But then... when we were adults, he gathered the family together, acknowledged his wrongdoings, and apologized for his actions when we were growing up. He showed a vulnerability and remorsefulness we had never seen before. He asked if there was anything at all that we wanted to discuss about what he had done in the past. He then explained that the love of Jesus had changed his life. He told us he was deeply sorry for the pain he had caused. I erupted with tears of gratitude, relief, and joy.

Four months later I was blessed with a profound and precious moment I will forever remember. It was the last time he was ever in my home before passing away. As he was leaving, he walked out the front door, down the steps, paused, turned, and said, "I couldn't have asked for a better daughter." This is my example of a father's love and that's how your heavenly Father feels about you! You are His favorite son. You are His favorite daughter. We *all* are His favorites! Nothing can separate us from His love. "For I am persuaded that neither death nor life, nor angels nor principalities nor powers, nor things present nor things to come, nor height nor depth, nor any other created thing, shall be able to separate us from the love of God which is in Christ Jesus our Lord" (Romans 8:38–39).

Three of the most powerful forces on the planet: Acknowledge, Apologize, Forgive.

Endless Love of God

How Do I Experience God?

In the first section of the Bible, called the Old Testament, there's a story about a prophet (someone who hears from

God and speaks what they hear) named Elijah. He was on a mountainside in Israel and God displayed His mighty power by sending fire to burn up some wet wood. Elijah and everyone there witnessed the miracle. They saw and had every reason to believe in God's power and protection. But an evil woman named Jezebel threatened Elijah, and he got so scared he ran away into the wilderness to hide;

> And when he saw that, he arose and ran for his life,
> and went to Beersheba. . . But he himself went a
> day's journey into the wilderness, and came and sat
> down under a broom tree. And he prayed that he
> might die, and said, "It is enough! Now, Lord, take
> my life, for I am no better than my fathers!"
> (1 Kings 19:3–4 NKJV)

This man was so scared that he ran away and wanted to die. A tad emotional, right? When we are an emotional wreck God is still with us like he was with Elijah. And then what did God do? In spite of his fear and running away, God sent an angel to feed and care for him:

> Then as he lay and slept under a broom tree,
> suddenly an angel touched him, and said to him,
> "Arise and eat." Then he looked, and there by his
> head was a cake baked on coals, and a jar of water.
> So he ate and drank, and lay down again.
> (1 Kings 19:5–6)

What do we learn from Elijah's plight? In the midst of our fear and turmoil, God is always with us. Through the tough times of my wilderness seasons, I learned to:

~ Identify and talk about how I feel.
~ Pay attention to emotional triggers.
~ Ask God to help me with my emotions.
~ Turn the emotions over to God.
~ Trust God to be there for me.
~ Look for God to be there.

God helps us go from an emotional wreck to an emotional rock.

Sharing with God or Jesus how we feel isn't complicated. Simply ask. He wants to help. "Hey God! Hey Jesus! Hey Holy Spirit! Help me with these feelings of hurt and anger. I give them to you. I release them to you. Show me what to do with them." Many times during the wilderness my cry was, "Help me!"

"And it is impossible to please God without faith. Anyone who wants to come to him must believe that God exists and that he rewards those who sincerely seek him" (Hebrews 11:6 NLT).

God's endless love is a path out of the wilderness.

How do we experience God?

~ Through that "little voice" in our head

~ Through His words in the Bible

~ Through the words of others

~ Through events around us

~ Even through movies, songs, and literature

There is nothing in the world more powerful than when the Creator of the universe shows Himself to us. He's here. Seek Him, and you will find Him.

"If you look for me wholeheartedly, you will find me." (Jeremiah 29:13 NLT)

We have natural eyes, and we have spiritual eyes. When using our natural eyes to see the tangibles around us we can ask, "Is God in this situation or circumstance? Is He in this? God, if you are here in this, show me." Looking for God is an act of faith. Faith is a gift from God which allows viewing with our natural eyes to transition into seeing with "eyes" of our spirit. We seek and then we find.

God always cares about what we say and what we pray. What's important to us is important to Him—even the smallest details. During the divorce I called a close friend. I shared intimate, painful details and asked for prayer. She said, "That's important stuff. I feel guilty because I was here praying about my mundane septic system problems!"

No need for guilt. God cares about divorce, and He cares when septic systems are a problem. Feel free to share with Him anything and everything important to you.

> ## Regardless of what we've done, God never gives up on us!

How Do I Experience God's Love?

I've shared my physical wilderness seasons and how I got through them with prayer and trusting God, counselors, friends, and family. Would I have gotten through them without a belief in God and in His love? Perhaps. Did I get through them more easily by believing and receiving His love, mercy, counsel, and grace as reliable tools upon which I relied? Absolutely.

Observing Nature's Beauty

As mentioned, one of God's names is Creator. The marvel of creation presents itself each year when mourning doves nest at my front door. From early spring through summer what was once décor for plants becomes their home.

Through a large window from my sofa, where I like to read and write, I watch them house hunt, nest sit, feed their babies, and teach them to leave the nest. I've concluded these sweet creatures only do what they do by divine design. When baby doves are very young, the mom and dad go to the nest and feed them, but before they enter the nest, they make their mourning dove cooing sounds. The babies associate cooing with feeding.

The first year the doves nested I was concerned because mom and dad weren't around for an entire day. I thought maybe the babies had been abandoned. Being the now observant birdwatcher, I researched and learned that the parents leave for long periods to let the little ones get really hungry. As the babies mature, and the time comes to leave the nest, mom and dad sit on the ground and coo. If you want to eat, come and get it! This is how they learn to fly and leave home. The parent doves know the exact timing of going to the nest to feed the little ones or sitting on the ground and letting babies come to them. It's all part of the divine design:

> Therefore I say to you, do not worry about your
> life...Look at the birds of the air, for they neither sow
> nor reap nor gather into barns; yet your heavenly
> Father feeds them. Are you not of more value than
> they? (Matthew 6:25–26 NKJV)

Ask Him to Show Up

God loves us unconditionally, and nothing, yes nothing, we do will separate us from this love. God may not be pleased with some of our actions (maybe we're not either), but that never changes or affects His love for us. Here is one of my favorite verses in the entire Bible:

> So now I live with the confidence that there is nothing in the universe with the power to separate us from God's love. I'm convinced that his love will triumph over death, life's troubles, fallen angels, or dark rulers in the heavens. There is nothing in our present or future circumstances that can weaken his love. There is no power above us or beneath us—no power that could ever be found in the universe that can distance us from God's passionate love, which is lavished upon us through our Lord Jesus, the Anointed One! (Romans 8:38–39 TPT)

We're open. We seek. We hear. As we open our spirit to a personal relationship with God, we will hear Him through that "small still voice." When we desire to know Him, then we see Him. He will show up!

Benefits of a Personal Relationship with God

"Just have faith and hope and everything will be okay." How tired are we of hearing that advice? How do I have faith and hope when I'm hurting, when I've lost my best friend, when I can't pay the bills, or when I've been told I have a life-threatening illness? I just want to veg out and sit in my misery. That's one option. The other is choose to deal with the situation, navigate the wilderness misery, and take steps to move beyond it.

I went through much of life with smatterings of faith and hope—a little here, a little there. Eventually I grasped how to put faith into action and be hopeful, even during super stressful times. *Faith* and *hope* were useless words to me until I came to understand what they really meant and, more importantly how to apply them.

Faith – Seeing is Believing vs. Believing is Seeing

A friend said, "Hope is an exhaustive subject." Yes, there are many aspects and characteristics of hope, so let's simplify things. What is hope? How do I get it?

During seasons of illness, I had to be intentional in choosing faith and hope for better health. It was either that or wallow in self-pity and give up. Giving up wasn't an option, so my first step was to identify why I had health issues. Next, I worked out an action plan to improve my health. This included doctors, holistic practitioners, essential oils, nutritional supplements, physical alignment (therapeutic massage, chiropractic, physical therapy), and exercise. It also included a spiritual action plan that included a deep dive into spiritual counseling relevant to forgiveness and repentance (being sorry and resolving to change). My faith and hope for better health were really there, but I had to have an action plan for my healing to come forth.

Faith is marginal or basically useless unless we activate it and participate in what we want to see happen. "Faith divorced from good works is phony" (James 2:20 TPT). Two simple workings to stir our faith, hopes, and desires into action are writing and speaking. Writing and speaking our hopes and desires increases the possibility they will become reality.

On an iconic, sunny, Florida morning, with ocean breezes gently blowing and sand under our feet, my father, stepmother (a.k.a. my bonus mom), and I were ocean fishing. Word up and down the beach was no one was catching fish. My stepmother, being the eternal optimist and believing if we declare a thing it will be established, started yelling out loud, "Frank Kristal [my father] will catch fish. We believe there are fish coming onto his line, and there will be fish caught by him this day!"

I'm not making this up. Not a single person on the entire beach caught fish that morning. Dad caught seven. Was that "luck," or was it my stepmother's faith in action? What she spoke happened. "Declare a thing and it will be established" (Job 22:28 NKJV).

We don't have to *hope* for the love of God. It is available to us 24/7/365. By faith we believe and receive this love. A primary component of love is giving. When we love someone, we give our time, our attention, our feelings, our hearts. Love is more than a feeling; it is an action. It requires a decision, and a commitment. How did God act on His love for us? We see it on signs at sporting events, on billboards, and all over the place:

"For God so loved the world he gave His only son so whoever believes in Him should not perish but have everlasting life" (John 3:16 NKJV).

God loved. God gave. God wants us with Him for all eternity.

Let's unpack this. God gave His only Son. If you don't believe in God, or if you don't believe Jesus is the Son of God, or if you don't believe in eternity or in heaven—this is where faith comes in. Faith is what we hope for, but we can't see. One aspect of faith is choosing what we believe. Some say seeing is believing. Not so much. In the spiritual realm believing is seeing. We see with our natural eyes, and we see with our spiritual eyes. Millions have faith God exists based on what's written in the Bible, the number-one best-selling book in the history of the world. As we read all those amazing God-inspired stories and miracles we have the opportunity to choose to believe them or not. When we choose to believe those accounts as true, and attach our faith to those beliefs, our spiritual being comes alive!

God is looking for us to have faith. He's looking for us to exercise and apply that faith by believing His truths even though we may not see them with our natural eyes. He wants us to believe, by faith, that He created everything. God wants us to open our spiritual eyes, heart, and mind and thereby experience His unconditional love.

 "Faith is the substance of things hoped for, the evidence of things not seen." (Hebrews 11:1 NKJV)

The word *substance* comes from the Greek word *hupostasis* meaning "a placing or setting under, a substructure or foundation." The word *evidence* comes from the Greek word *elengchos* meaning "a proof, or that by which a thing is proved or tested; conviction." Here's another version of Hebrews 11:1: "Now faith brings our hopes into reality and becomes the foundation needed to acquire the things we long for. It is all the evidence required to prove what is still unseen" (TPT). How?

~   Faith is a spiritual gift from God.
~   Ask for faith and receive it.
~   Faith and hope then reside in our spiritual being.
~   Faith is applied by adjusting our thoughts, our beliefs, and our desires so as to focus on what we cannot see with our natural eyes, but choose to believe.

Hope = Confident Expectation

Hope is the confident expectation that something will happen because we really, really want it. We're just feelin' it. We believe that "good thing" is on the way.

Hope recognizes what we want and expects it to happen. Hope believes our circumstances and situations will turn out for the best.

This concept is vital and bears repeating. Faith is the conviction of, or the belief in, something that we cannot see with our natural eyes. We hope for the very thing or circumstance that is the subject of our faith.

Hope begins with knowing what we desire and choosing what we believe.

Faith and Hope in Action

Since faith and hope are spiritual, they can't be intellectualized. Sometimes, thinking too much squelches faith and hope. Peter, one of the twelve disciples, provides us with a great example of overthinking faith. During a tumultuous storm on the Sea of Galilee, Jesus' followers were in a boat shaking with fear. In the distance they saw someone standing on the water. It was Jesus. They couldn't believe what they were seeing, but they knew it was real. Jesus told Peter to come out and join him. Do what? In an act of faith Peter stepped out of the boat and stood on the water with Jesus. Peter then looked around at the fierce wind and the huge waves. Suddenly, he was filled with fear and began to sink into the dark waters. He believed he could stand on the water, and he did, until he became afraid. Here's the lesson: fear diminishes faith. So, to expand your faith and have less fear, direct faith on the possibilities instead of what seems impossible.

God isn't looking for us to solve our problems. He's looking for us to have faith.

An ever-present reminder of this for me is the saying, "Fear knocked at the door. Faith answered. No one was there." Faith and fear cannot coexist. In every situation we have the ability to respond with one or the other, but not both. Aligning with God, Jesus and Holy Spirit creates a solid rock foundation against fearful thoughts trying to invade our mind, will and emotions. But how?

Faith is an opportunity to trust God to work things out for our highest and greatest good. What we think is best for us may not be His best for us. We ask and pray, and His answers may be yes, no, or wait. Maybe our timing isn't His timing. So how do we deal with that?

I've decided to trust God's plan rather than my own. It doesn't mean I sit around flipping through social media all day without purpose and goals. It *does* mean when I've prayed and asked for my heart's desires, I trust His timing, His plan, and His ways. For sure I have to conquer feelings of frustration and disappointment while waiting, but constantly affirming my belief that His ways are best helps me tremendously. This was my father's favorite scripture:

> For My thoughts are not your thoughts, nor are
> your ways My ways," says the Lord. "For as the
> heavens are higher than the earth, so are My ways
> higher than your ways, and My thoughts than your
> thoughts. (Isaiah 55:8–9 NKJV)

Faith and Our Words

The words we speak bring life, or the words we speak bring defeat. What we speak literally creates the atmosphere around us. Those very words build up or tear down. Words are so powerful they can change one's environment from positive to negative, or negative to positive.

Let's say you designed a plan to improve your health, which includes losing seven pounds in a month. You're making good choices with your diet and exercise, and you've already lost three pounds. It is more encouraging to say, "Yay! I'm losing weight" versus "I'm still four pounds overweight."

It is more life-giving and uplifting to say what you've accomplished instead of what you haven't.

In his book *What to Say When You Talk to Yourself,* Shad Helmstetter explains how our subconscious receives spoken words. A poignant example of this has stayed with me for years. A woman determined to quit smoking sits with friends puffing away on a cigarette and says, "I don't smoke. I am a nonsmoker." Obviously, this looks whack-a-doodle to those around her. Clearly, she is smoking, but by speaking out the words that she is a nonsmoker, her brain hears those words thereby increasing her ability to stop smoking. Instead of saying she's *trying* to quit smoking, she's saying she *has* quit smoking by stating out loud she is a non-smoker. This is faith in action, which comes with a caveat. This kind of faith is not a license to continue an undesired behavior or let go of a desired objective.

Seven months after Lance passed away, and just as I was getting a grip on my new life, my stepbrother and brother both died within one week. My family and I were in a wilderness season of incredible grief from losing three men in the family in such a short time. Being the administrative type, I accepted the responsibility of overseeing my brother's estate. Several weeks into the plethora of paperwork, phone calls, and emails, I was physically, mentally, and emotionally exhausted.

Remember the story of my friend who told me I should stop saying, "I'm overwhelmed?" Eventually, I recognized as long as I kept thinking that way, I was going to feel that way. When I flipped my thoughts to, "I can handle this. I will do the best I can," I felt much calmer.

Having a negative thought?
A positive thought

Several individuals criticized how I was handling things, and it was difficult dealing with the hurt feelings that came with their criticism. How did I deal with it? Here we are again full circle.

1. Acknowledge how you feel (disappointed, frustrated, fearful).

2. Check those feelings and perceptions with reality.

3. Explore and unpack those feelings.

4. Bring those feelings to God/Jesus/Holy Spirit.

5. Forgive those who hurt you.

Filling our mental and spiritual toolbox with faith and hope is key to conquering the wilderness.

Faith and Finances

At one point, my life had not come close to what I had envisioned. Disappointment was an intruder. I believed my destiny and calling was to be an entrepreneur, investor, and financier of businesses, ministries, and missions. I accomplished that... until all the money was gone.

I had not lived on a day-to-day survival budget since my college days. The financial crunch was terribly stressful, and by then I knew there was only one thing to do. I turned to God, His Word, His wisdom, and His counsel. I had to redirect my focus away from what was lost, both the tangible and intangible, and make a permanent, willful decision to take charge of my thoughts and emotions.

During the early morning hours my brain was like a washing machine agitator tossing around all sorts of emotions as I stressed about paying this bill and that bill. My thoughts directed my emotions; fear, stress, worry, and anxiety tried to sneak in. Sometimes to drive away the negative, fearful thoughts, I literally put my hand on my head and said, "I bring my thoughts under the authority of Holy Spirit!" I needed to drive out the negative thoughts and tap into faith and hope.

Remember the scripture in Philippians about being content? Well, it gave me much comfort and a reality check during that wilderness. Here it is in another translation.

> I'm not telling you this because I'm in need, for I have learned to be satisfied in any circumstance. I know what it means to lack, and I know what it means to experience overwhelming abundance. For I'm trained in the secret of overcoming all things, whether in fullness or in hunger. And I find that the strength of Christ's explosive power infuses me to conquer every difficulty. (Philippians 4:11–13 TPT)

These verses summed up where my life was at that time. I had abundance and now was experiencing lack. Anytime my mind went into "pity party" mode over losing a relationship, losing my financial stability, having a condo instead of a house, and not being able to help others—stop, stop, stop I commanded myself! I would pause for a thought-based reality check and look around at what I did have. Some days I would get up in the morning and change my affirmations by saying, "I have enough food for today. I have enough clothes to wear. I have a beautiful home. I have a car with gas in it. The bills are paid for today. I have what I need for today."

"Refuse to worry about tomorrow,
but deal with each challenge that
comes your way, one day at a time.
Tomorrow will take care of itself."
(Matthew 6:34 TPT)

Faith and Fear

Faith and fear have a common attribute. Faith calls us to believe in a positive, future thing not yet established. Fear wants us to believe in future negative things not yet established. However, there is quite a difference between the two. Faith lifts us up, emboldens us and gives us the confidence to move forward. Fear paralyzes as it triggers the release of negative emotions causing us to think our situation is hopeless.

There are people who have more than we have, and there are those who have less. There are those who appear to be more talented and gifted, and there are those who appear less gifted. There are those with bigger homes, and there are those with smaller ones. To remain peaceful, I cannot wish for nor covet what others have. Jealousy is bad news.

Previously I wrote about the mind-will-emotion connection. When we feel disappointment we can choose to dwell and sink in it like quicksand, or we can actively and purposely work through it. Given the financial disappointment I was experiencing, I needed to decide whether I was going to trust God or not. If I was going to trust Him I needed to act like it. I learned *how* to put faith and trust into action. I do this through:

~ Prayer, both alone and with friends.
~ Reading encouraging words from the Bible and other books.
~ Attending uplifting conferences and gatherings.
~ Filling my mind with the truth of the following verse:

"Keep your thoughts continually fixed on all that
is authentic and real, honorable and admirable,
beautiful and respectful, pure and holy, merciful and
kind. And fasten your thoughts on every glorious
work of God, praising him always."
(Philippians 4:8 TPT)

Implementing those choices shifted me from disappointment and discouragement to a place of hope and trust. Now, when I saturate my soul and spirit with the truth of anything and everything from the Word of God, my heart and spirit become peaceful and content. This is vital to how I conquer the wilderness.

The words and stories in the Bible
help us get through tough times.

Exercise the Faith Muscle

What's really cool about redirecting our thoughts and focusing on hope is that the more we do it, the more our faith increases! It's like exercising a muscle. The more you use your faith, the stronger it gets. I prayed a ton over every single investment and donation. My desire was to do only what God wanted. Did I hear accurately? I don't know for certain. But what I do know is my decisions were based on what I believed I was hearing. If I was off base, I earnestly and conscientiously did my very best. If I missed the mark I've asked His forgiveness, and I've been forgiven. I also had to forgive myself and move on. I couldn't get stuck in woulda shoulda coulda land!

What if an exercise of my faith, even after making those "bad" decisions, was to believe there was a purpose and it was part of my destiny to awaken me to many spiritual truths laying the foundation for this book? Now, there's a thought-provoking question. By exercising our faith God can take the worst wilderness and use it for His purposes.

God Understands

This is amazing. God understands. He understands your discouragements and your disappointments. He understands your hurts, frustrations and fears. Not only does He understand, He cares a ton about you and doesn't judge! With Him there is nothing off limits for prayer and conversation. God's love and the love of Jesus heals all of life's traumas. When choosing to trust them, a reciprocal love exchange takes place driving away fear, anxiety and frustrations. Without all those challenging emotions tying you up, you are better equipped to conquer and learn from your wilderness. And then get ready as the path to joy has now been opened! Here is the evidence:

"I have told you these things so that
My joy and delight may be in you,
and that your joy may be made full
and complete and overflowing."
(John 15:11 AMP)

Dealing with Disappointment

The Bible is filled with God's promises. When reading them I experience peace, fulfillment, and contentment. Satisfaction comes from Him and His Word not stuff, people, or more vacations. When we take every thought, hope, and dream to Him, God then works all things together for our best interest.

A reality of life—there *are* disappointments and delays. Day after day, year after year of challenges and delays might lead to discouragement. During the waiting, it may seem impossible to continue hoping, but hope is a matter of choice. Reflecting on and learning more about why disappointment is present, and then using the *Trusted Tools* are keys for having hope in wilderness seasons.

Perhaps you've hoped and prayed for a true love relationship, a child, a job promotion, or healed family relationships. When it doesn't happen in your timing, the disappointment feels real. Prolonged disappointment leads to unbelief, doubt, and discouragement. Unless we move out of those places, we could feel stuck, bitter, and even angry.

When I'm disappointed, I process what's going on with someone whose input I respect and trust. A friend's insight into how I feel helps me work through those feelings. Once I do, it makes accepting the delay easier. I can then intentionally respond with my will and make effective choices.

"Hope deferred makes the heart sick, but a longing fulfilled is a tree of life" (Proverbs 13:12 NIV). When hope has been deferred, depression and anxiety may try to arise. Delay is not always a no. Waiting is an opportunity to trust. The response to the request or desire could be not yet. If what you hope for still doesn't happen, then ask Is that hope realistic and in alignment with God's best for me? There is no right or wrong answer. This is where patience and discernment come in and an opportunity for a conversation between you and God.

TOOLBOX

- ¤ Describe your relationship with your earthly father. How does this influence you today? How does this influence your view of the heavenly Father?

- ¤ If you would like to experience the love of God, what does this look and feel like to you? Are you able to believe and receive that He loves you regardless of what you've done in the past? Why or why not?

- ¤ List all of those things that you are hoping for at this moment. What are the desires of your heart? What do you want to see manifest in your life? What would you like to see happen? Consider all possibilities: material, health, relational, family, career, spiritual, emotional, and anything else you desire in your life. Paint a picture of what your life looks like with more faith and with more hope.

◻ On your list, what personal steps will increase
   your chance of your hopes materializing if
   you put some action into it? For example,
   if you are hoping for a new job, have
   you started searching for one? Have you
   submitted resumes? Have you let the people
   who can help you know you are looking?

◻ Is there something in your life you want to
   give over to God? Is there something with
   which you want help?

CHAPTER 8

OUR DESIRES AND A DIVINE PLAN

What if we trusted God to know what's best? As your Creator, He knows the number of days you will live and the hairs on your head (that's in the Word). He knows you inside and out. Can you consider the possibility that His way will bring you more happiness, contentment, joy, and fulfillment than anything you could try yourself? Dare to believe what He says!

Having outlived two husbands, I hoped to marry again. Many years later, I was still single and I didn't understand why. I prayed. I declared it. I decreed it. I felt like I was in a holding pattern. I have girlfriends in their forties, fifties, and sixties who have never been married but really want to marry. Here's where I found peace.

> Keep trusting in the Lord and do what is right in His eyes. Fix your heart on the promises of God and you

will dwell in the land, feasting on his faithfulness.
Find your delight and true pleasure in Yahweh, and
he will give you what you desire the most. Give God
the right to direct your life, and as you trust him
along the way you'll find he pulled it off perfectly!
(Psalm 37:3–5 TPT)

Created for Relationship

Our identity in and relationship with
God is a **key** wilderness tool.

The wilderness is a time and a place where you can
become more like God. Say what? God is multidimensional,
multifaceted, and infinite. God is light. God is grace. God is
mercy. He says, "I am who I am" (Exodus 3:14 NKJV). This
means He is self-sufficient in and of Himself and doesn't need
anyone or anything to be God. He is the one and only Almighty
God. He is Spirit. We are not God, but we are made in His
image. We can't *be* God, but we can be like Him when we open
our spirit and allow His Spirit, Holy Spirit, to reside in us.

Why are we here on earth? What's our purpose? To have a
family, make money, help other people, save the planet? Maybe
some of that, but ultimately we are created for a beautiful,
wonderful, all fulfilling purpose: to be in relationship with God,
Jesus and Holy Spirit.

Healthy Dependence

With my finite brain I can't fully understand the *omniscient* (all-knowing), *omnipresent* (everywhere), and *omnipotent* (all-powerful) nature of God's divine being. Activating my spirit I choose faith, choose to believe in Him, choose to believe what the Bible says about Him, and believe what He says about you and me.

It's amazing that the Creator of the Universe cares about me! He cares about *you*! Because He cares so much about your eternal life (our body, soul, and spirit go somewhere after this earthly life) He sent Jesus, His Son, to earth to perform miracles, to show us how to love others, and then to die for all our sins (all the dumb stuff we did, we still do, and will do). God did all of that and so much more, so we can depend on Him and thereby experience a glorious, magnificent eternity beyond our wildest imaginations. That's what I'm talkin' about!

Eternity

My worldview changed forever when I read a certain book. It unpacked my earthly life from the spiritual viewpoint of eternity. My head can't comprehend forever and ever and ever and ever. However, I do believe eternity is real, heaven is real, and so is someplace else.

Just as our physical life began in our mother's womb, our spiritual life began in the creative mind of God. You and I are spirit, soul and body. We are spiritual beings living in an earthly body. When our physical bodies are gone, we will have what's called a resurrected body. Our spirits and our resurrected bodies have an eternal destination, which will be one of two places—heaven or hell. Where our spirit and this resurrected body end up for eternity is a choice. Yes, here we are, back to that faith and choice thing. We choose to believe Jesus is the Son of God, a.k.a. Son of Man, or we don't. It's literally a life (heaven) or death (hell) decision.

During our short "flash in the pan" life on earth, the ultimate satisfaction is attained by allowing God to work through us and trusting His plans. How so? It begins with identity. Who am I? Who are you?

Identity

Our identity has everything to do with everything. Sounds redundant and it is, but it isn't. Altogether our mind, will, emotions, heart, and spirit make us human and there is more. Our identity is a part of our character and personality distinguishing us from everyone else. It's what makes me distinctly me and you distinctly you. It's your mind and thought processes and also your spirit. When you connect with and flow with your spiritual identity, snap! Who you are begins to make sense. Your life has a strong and solid foundation that can't be rocked. When you know your spiritual identity, you'll have the primary key to conquering the wilderness and all of life.

During the wilderness as we further discover, develop, and understand our identity, God leads us toward our purpose and destiny.

The Bible is full of stories about people who were tossed into pits, stuck in jail, fought in wars, and wandered in the desert for days, months, and years. Sounds like my life at times, and I've learned much from these wilderness wanderers and jail dwellers.

In Chapter 2 we read about the Israelites who were slaves in Egypt for four hundred years when God told Moses he was to get them out of there. Moses gathered those several million people, and they began their eleven-day journey. They were to possess the land God was giving them—their destiny and inheritance—which was on the other side of the desert. To bring order to the journey, and to the rest of their lives, He gave them the Ten Commandments as a guide for living.

The Israelites were impatient. They grumbled and complained. Done that. *Why is this happening to me? What's taking so long?* There was a consequence of their whining and not trusting God—eleven days turned into forty years. Today we have map apps which could have helped, but would it? Their attitudes and choices were the real problem.

God had a good plan for their future, and when they got their act together, they finally made it to the place where their purpose and destiny as a blessed nation could be fulfilled. Their identity emerged as free children of God, orchestrated by a heavenly Father who loved them and wanted to set them free from slavery. There was a plan. There was a purpose. There was a destiny.

Wilderness times are often filled with frustration, uncertainty and confusion. When I'm in that place I look for ways to make sense of the mess. I look for order in the chaos. Chaos nearly always precedes order. Sometimes I don't see order nor do I understand the wilderness, but I do know this: when I look for and focus on God's order, I am less stressed and more peaceful. I become a conqueror. So can you!

Faith and the promises of God produce a new identity. You are a child of God and His desire is for a relationship with you. "How do you know that?" you ask.

Because it's in the Book. The Bible is the divinely inspired word of God, and it says, "'I will be a true Father to you, and you will be my beloved sons and daughters,' says the Lord Yahweh Almighty" (2 Corinthians 6:18 TPT). (Yahweh is another name for God.)

Again, let's consider our earthly father and heavenly Father. If your biological father was a rough fellow, or maybe absent from the home, relating to a heavenly Father could be hard. But notice these particular words, *true Father*. Love is the essence of our true heavenly Father and His being. He is a loving Father:

> For here is the way God loved the world—he gave
> his only, unique Son as a gift. So now everyone who
> believes in him will never perish but experience
> everlasting life. (John 3:16 TPT)

God loves us to such a great extent that He gave the greatest gift in the history of the world: His Son, Jesus. What does it mean he "gave" His Son? Jesus became God in the flesh, in a human form, who died so that we may have eternal life. When we choose to believe this and when we ask God to forgive us (that's called repentance), then we will have eternal life—life forever in heaven. There came a poignant moment in my life when I came as close as my physical brain could process to understanding the immeasurable love of the Father.

For years I attended a weekend silent retreat in my home state of Michigan. Being the extrovert that I am, my friends and family couldn't believe I could be quiet for an entire weekend, but I loved it. I silently walked the ninety acres of wooded pathways as the cool fall breezes settled in, bringing a peaceful refreshing to my soul and spirit. A focal point of the retreat center was a large pond with a footbridge taking visitors to an island on which stood a life-size figure of Jesus on a cross. It was familiar: I saw it every year. But one year I saw it with new eyes and a new heart.

The year after my son, Alex, was born, as a new mom I was looking forward to my retreat time more than ever. Upon arrival at the retreat center I settled into my room, anticipating the serenity of that first walk around the beautifully manicured landscape. I flung open the back door of the retreat house and there it was, on the island, Jesus on the cross. I stood as still as that monument. I couldn't move.

"For God so loved the world" whizzed through my mind. It was shock and awe. For the past year, I had experienced a love for my son I barely had words to describe. My love was all encompassing, all embracing, and completely unconditional. I would do anything for him. "He gave His only Son," came to mind. I started to cry. What had become familiar suddenly was profound. God allowed His Son to be tortured, humiliated, and hung on a cross. His death and resurrection took on a new dimension. Why was this necessary?

"That whoever believes in him will have eternal life."

Why? So we would live forever in heaven with God, Jesus, Holy Spirit, the angels, and others who believe.

In that moment, while juxtaposing the love I had for my son with God's love for me, I realized I could not and would not ever be able to comprehend the massive love God has for me. I couldn't fathom putting my son to death so the world could be saved from the horror of hell. In that moment, I gave up trying to understand the limitless love of God, and I made a choice to receive it again in my heart.

Sometimes It Takes Time

Joseph was the youngest of twelve brothers and his dad's favorite, so much so that his dad made him an exquisite coat. Joseph's jealous brothers threw him into a pit and sold him into slavery. Joseph had a time of favor while a servant for Pharoah's captain of the guards, but after a false accusation he spent thirteen years in prison. After being in jail all those years, God rescued him, and he ended up being appointed the second most powerful man in Egypt.

Feel like you're in prison? Keep your hope! Your destiny is on the other side of the wall.

When we are intentional about seeing the purpose in our mess and when we are open to God's process, wilderness seasons bring alignment and order. Jesus is a great example of how God works in our wilderness. Right before Jesus went into a literal desert, he was baptized. What's baptism and why is this important? Because that's when God called Jesus, "My Beloved Son."

> When he had been baptized, Jesus came up immediately from the water; and behold, the heavens were opened to Him, and He saw the Spirit of God descending like a dove and alighting upon Him. And suddenly a voice came from heaven, saying, "This is My beloved Son, in whom I am well pleased." (Matthew 3:16–17 NKJV)

This story appears several times throughout the Bible, recorded by those who observed the baptism and heard the Father proclaim pleasure in His Son. And then, that divine moment was followed by a dark wilderness.

The Holy Spirit (more on him later) led Jesus into the dry, desolate desert. Jesus chose to follow. But what if he didn't? Well, the Word says Jesus always did what he saw the Father doing and always spoke what he heard the Father saying.

But what if we don't follow a divine leading? Instinctively we don't want wilderness experiences, or when we're in one we just want out. I didn't choose heartaches, pain, and hardships. Who would?

During my wilderness seasons I learned to earnestly search for answers as to what was going on in my body, mind, and soul and looked for any tiny bit of good during those tough times. I asked myself:

~ What can I learn about myself while I'm in this situation?

~ Is there a higher purpose I may not be seeing?

~ How can I grow emotionally, mentally, and spiritually from this situation?

~ What does God want to do in and through me in this wilderness?

Acceptance

When we accept our wilderness situation (although not indefinitely) and look for purpose, God is able to reveal the lessons He has for us. Here is an important caution about accepting one's wilderness. If you are in a situation that is physically, emotionally, sexually, or in any other way abusive or harmful, this must not be tolerated. If you are in such a situation it is imperative to reach out for help. Please seek professional assistance immediately so you can get to a place of physical and emotional safety. Resources are at the end of the book.

Developing Identity

Jesus was led by the Spirit into the wilderness to:

~ Fast and pray

~ Spend time with His Father

~ Be prepared to reveal His destiny

~ Be tempted by the devil

~ Overcome the devil

By natural appearances Jesus was alone, He appeared to be by Himself in the wilderness, but he was never spiritually alone. This is because God is omnipresent; He is everywhere all the time. I've given up trying to understand it—I have faith that it is the truth. We may be physically alone, but the Spirit of God is always present. God is a gentleman, and gives us a free will. We *choose* how close we become to Him as we exercise our free will.

After the desert, Jesus returned "in the power of the Spirit." What He did next demonstrated the power and purpose He developed while in His wilderness experience.

Jesus went to the synagogue where people gathered for study and prayer. He was handed the scroll (no bound books yet) with the reading for that particular day from the book of Isaiah. He stood and read:

> The Spirit of the Lord God is upon Me, Because the LORD has anointed Me To preach good tidings to the poor; He has sent Me to heal the brokenhearted, To proclaim liberty to the captives, And the opening of

the prison to those who are bound; To proclaim the
acceptable year of the LORD. (Isaiah 61:1–2 NKJV)

Many years later the disciple Luke wrote about that very day:

Then He [Jesus] closed the book, and gave it back
to the attendant and sat down. And the eyes of all
who were in the synagogue were fixed on Him. And
He said to them, "Today this Scripture is fulfilled in
your hearing." (Luke 4:20–21 NKJV)

Whoa! Jesus was telling them *He* was the one God sent to
preach, heal, proclaim liberty, and open the prison—the prison
of our soul and spirit. He declared His identity as their long-
awaited Messiah, the Savior of the world.

Catch this recap:

~ Jesus had just been in the desert.
~ He went into the synagogue.
~ He stood and read from the scroll of Isaiah with God's
teachings.
~ He said He was the one for whom they were waiting.

Jesus came out of the wilderness, and when He said, "Today
this Scripture is fulfilled in your hearing," He declared that
He was hope, freedom, new eyes for the blind, and freedom
for prisoners. He declared He was the Messiah. Jesus left his
heavenly position and took on the form as a man. This was His
identity and purpose on earth. Jesus' wilderness encounter was

profoundly transitional, moving Him toward His purpose and identity.

There is another aspect of Jesus' identity that is associated with "liberty for the captives" and "opening of the prison to those who are bound." Because we have a soul (mind, will, and emotions) and are human, we sin. No finger pointing here; we're not perfect. Here's what happened after Jesus died on the cross. They placed his dead and beaten body in a tomb, and three days later He was alive! He what? Yes, He was dead for three days and then He rose up out of that grave! That's what much of the world celebrates on Resurrection Sunday, which some call Easter. For 40 days Jesus appeared to His disciples and others before He ultimately ascended into heaven.

Jesus' resurrection proves His identity as the Son of God.

That same resurrection power is available to you. Jesus put what He has inside of you and me. Read on and grab it!

> I pray that you will continually experience the immeasurable greatness of God's power made available to you through faith. Then your lives will be an advertisement of this immense power as it works through you! This is the mighty power that was released when God raised Christ from the dead

and exalted him to the place of highest honor and
supreme authority in the heavenly realm!
(Ephesians 1:19–20 TPT)

Jesus came out of the wilderness with power and purpose. You can too.

The Attempt to Keep Us from Our Identity

When Jesus rose up out of the grave, He crushed Satan's
authority over all the earth. To this very day, that same devil is
the biggest, baddest being coming after us in the wilderness,
and all the time for that matter. Because of mankind's fallen
nature, the devil has some authority on the earth. That "destiny
destroyer" wants to take everything away from us, confuse us,
and make us miserable.

The Destiny Destroyer

During those forty days Jesus was hot, hungry, and thirsty.
Though He was one with God (they are one Spirit), He still had
a physical human body. Satan (the name means adversary), the
devil, showed up to tempt him. Talking about the devil makes
some people uncomfortable, but it's imperative to understanding
what is coming against you. He literally wants to make your life
miserable and even take you out. Having this knowledge is vital
to conquering the wilderness!

In the wilderness we're vulnerable and temptations ramp up. Satan, demons, and principalities are not Halloween-like figures in red costumes with pitchforks. They are spiritual beings. Knowing what they are and what they want to do gives us the number-one rule of warfare: know your enemy.

> Your hand-to-hand combat is not with human beings, but with the highest principalities and authorities operating in rebellion under the heavenly realms. For they are a powerful class of demon-gods and evil spirits that hold this dark world in bondage. (Ephesians 6:12 TPT)

Evil principalities try to keep us from happiness and joy, to keep us from hope and love, and to keep us in a dark, desolate wilderness. They want to keep us tied up, prevent us from fulfilling our purpose and destiny, and prevent us from God's appointed purposes. What's the main goal of Satan? To keep us from knowing our true identity as children of God. Satan wanted to keep Jesus away from His purpose and mission by tempting and distracting Him.

A few of the names of Satan:

Adversary

Counterfeiter

Devil

Evil One

Father of Lies

Ruler of this World and god of this Age

Lucifer

Ruler of the Kingdom of the Air

The Tempter

The Accuser of the Brothers (and sisters)

The Dragon

The Serpent

During wilderness times, we are vulnerable to people, places, and things trying to get us off course and keep us from fulfilling our destiny. Anxiety and fear are components of the enemy's agenda. Ignoring or not acknowledging the devil doesn't make him go away, nor will it make him stop bothering you. Be encouraged! Knowing *what's* coming at you gives you the *know-how* to overcome, so you can conquer temptations. "You are of God, little children, and have overcome them, because He who is in you is greater than he who is in the world" (1 John 4:4 NKJV). Let's make this clear.

When you make the choice to believe and receive Jesus in your heart, God is *in* you!

The same resource which helped Jesus helps us. We can do what Jesus did in resisting what we know is damaging to us. The devil tried to tempt Jesus three times and here's how He responded. Jesus spoke out loud the words of his Father as was written in the Old Testament scrolls. In the text below, first you'll read what the Old Testament (OT) says. Then you'll read what is written in the New Testament (NT), that Jesus quoted from the OT.

Get the devil out of your life by speaking out loud what God says!

OT: "So He humbled you, allowed you to hunger, and fed you with manna which you did not know nor did your fathers know, that He might make you know *that man shall not live by bread alone;* but man lives by every word that proceeds from the mouth of the LORD." (Deuteronomy 8:3 NKJV, emphasis added)

NT: When the devil told him to turn stones into bread Jesus said, *"Man shall not live by bread alone,* but by every word that proceeds from the mouth of God.'" (Matthew 4:4 NKJV, emphasis added).

~ ~ ~

OT: *"You shall not tempt the LORD your God."* (Deuteronomy 6:16 NKJV, emphasis added)

NT: When the devil told Him if he was the Son of God to jump and the angels would catch him, Jesus said, "It is written again, *'You shall not tempt the LORD your God.'"* (Matthew 4:7 NKJV, emphasis added)

~ ~ ~

OT: *"You shall fear the LORD your God and serve Him,* and shall take oaths in His name. You shall not go after other gods." (Deuteronomy 6:13–14 NKJV, emphasis added)

NT: When the devil offered him all the kingdoms of the world, Jesus said, "Away with you, Satan! For it is written, *'You shall worship the LORD your God, and Him only you shall serve.'"* (Matthew 4:10 NKJV, emphasis added)

~ ~ ~

What do we learn from these examples? Quoting the Bible kicks the devil out of your way! In addition to telling the devil to back off, Jesus was also encouraging Himself with God's word. When the wilderness battle ended, "the devil left Him, and behold, angels came and ministered to Him" (Matthew 4:11 NKJV). The subject of angels is a whole book in itself, and my favorite is *Angel Armies* by Dr. Tim Sheets. Angels are not fluffy, passive beings floating around on clouds. I get excited every time I open the pages of *Angel Armies*. Angels are the hands of God acting as mighty warriors battling spiritual darkness, protectors, and facilitators of our destiny.

Vulnerable Times

Wilderness seasons create voids. During times of hardship and heartache we can feel isolated in the wilderness of our thoughts. Something is missing. We don't feel good, so our instinct is to fill the void and ease the pain. That's when the temptation to mask the discomfort entices us into too much or perhaps too little. We become vulnerable to temptations.

Too much could include too much drinking, too much work, too much shopping or spending, too much social media, too much television, too much sexual indiscretion or pornography, too many drugs, or overeating. The enemy uses these masks and cover-up temptations to fill the empty and wounded places of the soul.

The opposite might occur as well. Instead of too much, one may retreat into too little. We feel unmotivated and don't feel like doing anything. We struggle to get through the routines of the day. We might withdraw, isolate, or become depressed. We disconnect from family and friends. All of these behaviors lead to an even greater void. We may be in such pain or trauma we wonder if it will ever end. It can and it will!

It's human nature to desire to feel balanced and well. We want to be happy. We want the loss and grief to go away. We want the wilderness to end. Applying the tools you have learned will help you get through it. At the same time awareness of what we're tempted to do in the wilderness and avoiding the undesirable temptations is a huge step.

Good Guilt and Unresolved Guilt

We've all felt guilty. We do or say something and then we're remorseful. Guilt is useful when it results in a correction of behavior and actions. It may lead us to apologize and turn away from shady behaviors. Guilt can be turned around by having the courage to do what may be difficult, by doing the right thing.

Unresolved guilt, constantly feeling badly about yourself, could lead to a loss of self-esteem, self-worth, and self-value.

Unresolved guilt is an identity stealer. When feelings of guilt were pervasive in my thinking, I had to:

~ Identify exactly what led to the guilt;

~ Decide what would resolve the guilt (apologizing, forgiving others or myself); and

~ Take appropriate action to correct and remedy any wrongdoing.

Shame

Guilt is behavior focused while shame is self-focused. Shame is a painful feeling of humiliation, embarrassment, or regret resulting from ongoing behavior, what we've done in the past, or what someone has done to us. It may arise from a sense of failure, inadequacy, or wrongdoing. Shame is when guilt becomes part of your identity—something God never designed you to have.

The tremendous shame my husband Lance felt from his pornography addiction made him react with outrageous anger. The constant hiding, sneaking, and covering up was exhausting. Devilish companions to shame, and common to many with anger issues are hurt, pride (fear of man—what do people think), and guilt.

If shame has a vice grip on your soul, it's virtually impossible to walk in the fullness of your identity and to feel good about yourself. Spiritual and professional counsel helps get to the core of the underlying issues. In the meantime, changing behaviors and declaring "Shame off" are initial steps.

Genesis is the first book of the Bible. In the first chapter, it says God made us in His image, male and female. God is spirit. So are we. Then God said, "Let Us make man in Our image, according to Our likeness; let them have dominion over the fish of the sea, over the birds of the air, and over the cattle, over all the earth and over every creeping thing that creeps on the earth. So God created man in His own image; in the image of God He created him; male and female He created them" (Genesis 1:26–27 NKJV).

Our spirit is the part of our being created to connect with God. Our spirit longs for this connection. God desires this connection. We were created for this connection. This connection is activated and comes fully alive when we believe in Jesus, and we enter into a relationship with Jesus and Holy Spirit. We choose the depth of the connection.

Then there's the enemy who will do anything to keep us from having this connection. He will try anything and everything to steal our identity. The enemy will use shame, guilt, addictions, and every vulnerability to keep us from knowing our identity as children of the Most High God. "Be well balanced and always alert, because your enemy, the devil, roams around incessantly, like a roaring lion looking for its prey to devour" (1 Peter 5:8–9 TPT).

That enemy who tempted Jesus in the desert didn't want Him to fulfill His purpose. He wanted to get Jesus off track. He tries to do the same with us. Satan wants to keep us in the dark about who we are. He wants to keep us all from knowing and experiencing the love of the Father, so we will not fulfill our purposes and destinies on earth, because when we understand who we are and whose we are, we have power and authority. Awareness of the devil's tricks and deceptions allows us to awaken to who we really are and to whom we truly belong.

When we are in Christ, we are a new creation; we take on His identity. "I can do all things through Christ who strengthens me" (Philippians 4:13 NKJV). Not some things. Not a few things. It says we can do *all* things through Christ because He is the one who strengthens us.

The devil doesn't want us to know **we** have the power to overcome him!

Identity Coming Alive

John, another of the disciples, wrote one of my favorite verses:

> I tell you this timeless truth: The person who follows me in faith, believing in me, will do the same mighty miracles that I do—even greater miracles than these because I go to be with my Father!
> (John 14:12 TPT)

Jesus said what? When we follow and believe in Him, we can do the same and even greater miracles than He did! Jesus told the disciples to do what He did. He healed the sick, raised the dead, and cast out demons. How's that for an identity display? That's the identity available to you, to me, to everyone. Believe and receive.

If you don't remember anything from this book know this:

There is one true God, the father of Abraham, Isaac, Jacob, and Jesus, who loves every person, who loves you.[5] *Nothing you do or don't do changes His love for you.*

God's love is unconditional, freely given, and full of grace and mercy.

How can God love us when we've been bad? Sometimes, like most parents, He disciplines us the way He disciplined the Israelites in the desert when they misbehaved, a.k.a. when they were sinning. We discipline to teach our children right from wrong. When my son acted up and was unruly, I corrected him. I may not have liked his behavior, but I still loved him. That's how it is with God.

You are a child of God, and He loves you. This is your identity. Receiving the love of God is a choice. As I said, I can't fully understand how He always loves me regardless of my actions. He may not like my behavior, but He still loves me. I don't quite get it, but I believe it.

God even loves those who are mean, lie, cheat, and steal. Here's the scoop: they are His to deal with. He doesn't like actions against His Word and will, but He still loves the person, because love is His essence.

God's love conquers the wilderness of our soul.

If our trust is in humans, we are bound for disappointment because, well, we're human and so are they. We're not perfect; they're not perfect. We're all a work in progress. We're learning and growing and trying to do the best we can at navigating this thing called life. Our hearts are 100 percent secure in God.

Relationship with the Trinity

> Go therefore and make disciples of all nations,
> baptizing them in the name of the Father, the Son
> and of the Holy Spirit. (Matthew 28:19 NKJV)

Upon reading Chapter 3 you understand communication is foundational to every relationship. Our relationships are with people, with ourselves, and when we so choose, with God, Jesus, and Holy Spirit. God, Jesus, and Holy Spirit are often referred to as the Trinity. Although the word *trinity* is not in the Bible, the concept exists. Our mode of communicating with them is like with anyone else: we talk, we listen.

God is a divine spirit existing in three persons: the Father, the Son (Jesus), and Holy Spirit. Each person of the Trinity is fully God, and our relationship with each of them is unique.

When we communicate with God we speak to the entire Trinity. We communicate with God through prayer, as we seek guidance, express appreciation, or make requests. To effectively communicate with Him we read, study, and memorize His Word.

Volumes of information exist on ways we communicate with God. Here are a few:

1. Through the "small, still" voice in our head from His Spirit

2. Through His words in the Bible

3. Through other people (this takes discernment)

4. Through circumstances

5. Through prayer

> When we pray, we are talking to God. When we are quiet, we are listening to God.

"But I don't know God. I can't see God. I can't feel God." I get it. I saw, felt, and found Him when I passionately and purposely asked Him to show up. To see God, we have to look for Him. "You will seek Me and find Me, when you search for Me with all your heart" (Jeremiah 29:13 NKJV).

When we communicate with Jesus we are talking to the second person of the Trinity. Jesus took on human form; He is both fully God and fully human. Communication with Jesus develops a personal relationship with Him as we express our love for Him. Why love Him? Because He died on the cross so that we may have eternal life.

When we communicate with Holy Spirit, we address the third person of the Trinity. Holy Spirit reveals to us our wrongdoings (sin; the wrong stuff we do) and guides us into all truth. Holy Spirit communicates on our behalf to the Father, especially when we don't know how to pray or are weary.

> All this I have spoken while still with you. But the
> Advocate, the Holy Spirit, whom the Father will
> send in my name, will teach you all things and will
> remind you of everything I have said to you.
> (John 14:25-26 NIV)

During my wilderness times when I was weary, exhausted, and so frustrated I didn't know how to pray, I said, "Holy Spirit. I'm tired and I don't even know how to pray about this. Please pray on my behalf."

To someone who does not believe in the Trinity it may seem far-fetched to talk with spiritual beings who don't talk back. But wait! Believing in and communicating with them, will result in you *hearing* them.

Why? Remember, we are spiritual beings having a human experience while navigating through life in a human body. We have a spirit, and our spirit connects to the Spirit of the Divine Creator of the universe—to God.

"But what if it feels fake to have a conversation with someone we're not exactly sure is there much less listening?" When I was a child, my maternal grandmother helped me get past this. She said, "Faith is a choice." I paused, processed what she said, and then realized I had to contend for faith.

Engaging in a conversation with a being we can't see or touch requires faith; and the release of faith is a spiritual dynamic, not merely a cognitive decision or an intellectual conclusion. Choices are cognitive decisions. Decisions happen in our head. Faith operates in our spirit, soul, will and heart. Faith is a gift from God:

> For it is by grace [God's remarkable compassion and favor drawing you to Christ] that you have been saved [actually delivered from judgment and given eternal life] through faith. And this [salvation] is not of yourselves [not through your own effort], but it is the [undeserved, gracious] gift of God.
> (Ephesians 2:8 AMP)

Our life experiences, heredity, upbringing, relationships, and environment influence what we currently believe and what we will choose to believe in the future. When I made the choice to believe in God, my heart and spirit were open to hearing Him. I communicated with Him.

A mustard seed is one of the tiniest seeds on the planet. Jesus told His disciples,

> Assuredly, I say to you, if you have faith as a mustard
> seed, you will say to this mountain, "Move from
> here to there," and it will move; and nothing will be
> impossible for you. (Matthew 17:20 NKJV)

Not feeling like you have much faith? Then just act like you do. Act as if you believe and guess what? You will begin to believe. Take small steps in talking with God, reading what He says, being quiet, and listening.

God the Father and Master Designer

We've mentioned a few of the characteristics of this loving, merciful, full of grace heavenly Father, but how do we enter into a relationship with Him? Believe He exists. Believe He can hear you. Believe He wants to help you. "For I, the LORD your God, will hold your right hand, saying to you, 'Fear not, I will help you'" (Isaiah 41:13 NKJV).

Reading what the Bible says about God helps us to know Him. Prayer and being quiet develops our relationship with Him. When we respond to what is in His word, our spirits grow and develop, and we actually can become more like Him. Now there's a *wow* moment! That doesn't mean "being" God. It means because we are created in His image, we can take steps toward taking on His characteristics, which may involve aligning our values, behaviors, and morals to reflect His nature. This includes being honest and having integrity, kindness, and forgiveness, and treating others with love.

Jesus, the Son of God and Redeemer

Communication with God and Jesus are similar. Jesus said, "My sheep hear My voice, and I know them, and they follow Me" (John 10:27 NKJV).

So, now we're sheep? Sheep are helpless and not so smart; they need a shepherd. When Jesus referred to us as sheep, he wasn't saying we're brainless. But we do need direction and guidance to give us strength and help us find our way. There is a video on YouTube called "My Sheep Hear My Voice [AMAZING TEST] - John 10:27." It's about people calling to a flock of sheep hoping the four-legged fluffy ones will come running. Since the sheep don't recognize the strange voices they totally ignore the people and continue grazing in the field. When their shepherd approaches and calls to them, their little heads pop up, they all stop eating, and off they go running toward their master. They recognized the master's voice and so can we.

Trips to Israel are memorable highlights in my life. One year I didn't feel led to sign up for a particular Holy Land tour. It turned out many of my close friends were going, and I was really sad. The day before they left, I said out loud, "I really want to go." Instantly I heard a still small voice in my head say, "I know you do, honey."

Was that me talking to myself or was it the voice of God, Jesus, or Holy Spirit? I didn't know for sure, but I did know and appreciate in that moment hearing those words lifted me out of sadness. I believe God acknowledged my feelings; He truly knows how we feel.

Jesus died for our sins and was resurrected. When we receive this truth and believe in Him, we then live forever in a glorious eternity.

Saying we are sorry for our sins is not meant to be a guilt trip. Instead, it sets us free from the guilt of wrongdoing. Telling God we're sorry is called repentance. It means to change our mind, to make an about-face, and turn away from what we've done or said. We turn from our old sinful ways in another direction; that direction is a turn toward God.

Want to hear something truly amazing? When He died on the cross Jesus took our sins for us! His death redeemed us and set us free from our sins. He gave His life so that we could live forever in heaven.

Think of writing a note to Jesus on a dry erase board which includes all your sins, misbehaviors, and bad actions and words. Then with His divine eraser Jesus wipes the board clean. That my friend is redemption for our sins. We identify what we've done wrong, we repent, and we're forgiven. It's done. It's over. Release of guilt. Release of shame. And there's more. At the same time He takes on our sins, Jesus' righteousness is attributed to us! We put on His righteousness. On one hand he takes our sins, and on the other hand we take on his righteousness. Best deal on planet earth, would you agree?

Jesus meets us when we are weak and vulnerable. Acknowledging our innermost thoughts and feelings might make us feel vulnerable. Vulnerability is often associated with weakness. But that is not so. Society tends to shun weakness, but a deep dive into our innermost thoughts and weaknesses can produce power! Let me explain by quoting the apostle Paul: "I refuse to boast unless it concerns my weaknesses" (2 Corinthians 12:5 TPT).

Why would anyone boast of weakness? In this case, Paul knew what His friend and teacher, Jesus, had said: "My power finds its full expression through your weakness" (2 Corinthians 12:9 TPT).

The power of Jesus manifests through our weakness.

Jesus identifies with our weakness. "Yet God sent us his Son in human form to identify with human weakness" (Romans 8:3 TPT).

This gets even better.

"And in a similar way, the Holy Spirit takes hold of us in our human frailty to empower us in our weakness" (Romans 8:26 TPT).

What does it look like to be empowered in weakness? When we get to the end of our rope and when we are tired and weak, we can turn to Jesus for His power. "Be supernaturally infused with strength through your life-union with the Lord Jesus. Stand victorious with the force of his explosive power flowing in and through you" (Ephesians 6:10 TPT). The explosive power of Jesus is available to flow through us. The path out of the wilderness is infused with the explosive power of Jesus. At our weakest, most vulnerable, and most transparent times, Jesus is there to guide us. When we ask, He walks beside us through the dark times, the brighter times, and through *all* times.

Our Spirit and Holy Spirit

Another name for Holy Spirit is Holy Ghost. No, not like the creepy ghosts in *Ghost Busters*. He is the Holy Ghost, Holy Spirit, the One connected to God—part of the Trinity. Holy Spirit is a comforter. He helps us, teaches us, and gives us joy in the wilderness. Volumes of information exist on a relationship with Holy Spirit so let's simplify:

~ God reveals Himself through Holy Spirit.

~ Holy Spirit speaks to us.

~ Holy Spirit connects us to the mind of Jesus Christ.

~ Holy Spirit reveals spiritual truths to those who believe in God and Jesus.

We can experience and discover peace in the wilderness when our spirit connects to Holy Spirit. When we are open to the presence of Holy Spirit, we activate our spiritual eyes and ears. Through Holy Spirit, our spirit can understand the immeasurable essence of God. Let that sink in for a moment.

We can talk to and hear the voice of the Creator of the universe through Holy Spirit. God has a plan, and it is for our good. Our relationship with Holy Spirit allows us to see and understand that plan.

The Center of God's Will

Would you believe God's will is all about love? Is your will the same or different? If different, can you accept God's will over our own? To do so takes trust.

Trust in Him

Trust requires a level of safety. When I trust someone with my heart, I need to feel and believe he or she is an emotionally safe person for me. This means I am at ease and comfortable in sharing my most intimate thoughts and emotions without fear of judgment or criticism. No matter how rough the waters, I know I'll remain clear of rocks and turbulent waves when I'm with that person.

But of course, we're all human and stuff happens. People hurt us, betray us, and offend us whether intentionally or unintentionally. Not so with God.

"Trust in the Lord with all your heart and lean not on your own understanding" (Proverbs 3:5 NKJV). Though I don't fully comprehend the magnitude of God, I do know He has revealed Himself to me because I trust Him with my heart (the soul/spirit thing) and don't try to understand Him in my head.[6]

20 Powerful Reasons To Trust God

1. God's Word is absolutely and completely true.

2. He does not lie.

3. He never changes in His being.

4. He is consistent.

5. He never changes His plans or purposes.

6. He has never failed to fulfill His Word.

7. He is sovereign over all things.

8. He is infinitely wise.

9. He is faithful.

10. He is infinitely loving.

11. He gave His Son for us.

12. He is completely just.

13. He has wonderful plans for His people.

14. He will make you like Christ.

15. He is infinitely good.

16. He is always good to His children.

17. He won't leave you.

18. He cares for you.

19. He will never let you go.

20. He is with you.

God desires the best for us because He unconditionally, absolutely, positively loves us. For me a daily test of believing His love for me is trusting His will is better than my own. How do I know what that will is? This is another complex subject so I'll focus on three aspects of God's will: (1) His perfect will, (2) His permissive will, and (3) His discerned will.

What is God's perfect will? There are many scriptures about God's will, and here are two of my favorites:

> "For I know the plans I have for you," says the Lord. "They are for good and not for evil, to give you a future and a hope." (Jeremiah 29:11 TLB)

> Never doubt God's mighty power to work in you and accomplish all this. He will achieve infinitely more than your greatest request, your most unbelievable dream, and exceed your wildest imagination! He will outdo them all, for His miraculous power constantly energizes you. (Ephesians 3:20 TPT)

These verses reveal the heart of God. He has a plan for us, that plan is for our good, and He will work in us to accomplish His plan. This is just a small part of His heart for us.

Now, let's look at what His plan is not. The permissive will of God is what is allowed even though it is not in alignment with His word and His plan for us. For example, it is never

God's will for someone to be emotionally, physically, or sexually abused. He commands us to love one another. But because evil exists and people have a free will, when abuse happens, it grieves the heart of God. So why doesn't He stop it? That's a question for which unfortunately I don't have an answer, but I do know our prayers can change situations.

How do I know His will for me? I discern and perceive God's will for me through reading His word thereby gaining wisdom, knowledge, and understanding. Let's have grace with ourselves knowing we do the best we can when our motives and intentions are right with Him.

The Desires of Your Heart

But what about me and the desires of my heart? When I look at what the Bible says about the heart it's, well, unusual. One thing it says is the heart is deceitful, and then it also says, God looks on our heart. We read about King David asking God to, "Create in me a clean heart." One "how-to" answer is, "Delight yourself in the LORD and He will give you the desires of your heart" (Psalm 37:4 NKJV).

What does delight mean? It means to find peace and fulfillment in Him. How? Even though we look around and life may not be what we expected or hoped for, we can remain grateful and content through it all. When God is the focus of our heart, when He becomes the foremost desire of our heart, we become conquerors in the wilderness.

TOOLBOX

- Understanding the magnitude of God is challenging for our human brains however, what if you seek to know Him by exercising your faith and asking Him to reveal himself to you? Do you dare to choose faith and believe He wants a relationship with you?

- What would change in your life if you trusted God and the possibility of His divine plan for your life?

- Have you ever discussed eternity with anyone? Is there someone with whom you would like to have such a conversation?

- Did you ever experience a wilderness season and consider how it may have moved you toward your purpose and destiny?

- Have you ever discussed the devil with anyone? Did you know the devil seeks to destroy you? Can you believe you have the authority to get him out of your life? If so, would your exercise of such authority help you in a future wilderness encounter? This is a significant leap out of the wilderness.

¤   What did you do during vulnerable times in your life? Given what you've learned so far, are there things you will do differently in the future?

¤   Are you ready to embrace a relationship with God, Jesus and Holy Spirit? Why or why not?

CHAPTER 9

OUT OF THE WILDERNESS

Live in His Love

My desire to know, to see, and to feel God was followed by putting my faith into action. You see, I have faith and trust that God's love is true, and I choose to live in that reality. As an example, it's similar to how we acquire and associate with our friends. We decide based on a variety of reasons which friends we have in our lives and which friends we choose to exclude. Some are "in" and some are "out." And there are times when others decide whether they want *us* in or out.

This decision making doesn't happen with God. We are always in with Him! He doesn't *need* us (He has the whole universe), but because of his unconditional love He *desires* a relationship with each and every one of us. Regardless of what we've done, He freely gives us His love. In this relationship we are able to hear and receive what He knows, which can be applied to our lives and circumstances. When you activate your faith and open your heart to a relationship with God you come to know:

~ His desire is to guide you.

~ His desire is to protect you.

~ His desire is to help you fulfill your purpose and destiny.

~ His desire is to heal you.

~ His desire is to comfort you.

~ His desire is to take you into the place of your highest calling.

~ His desire is to be in an intimate relationship with you.

~ His desire is to love you fully.

And all He asks of you is that you allow Him to be your heavenly Father and friend.

Trusting God's Timing

I'm not saying life will suddenly become easy, but I am saying it can be *easier* when we consider our perceptions. God doesn't promise to eliminate all our tough times, but He does promise He will be with us through all of them. One of the last things Jesus told his disciples was that in the world there would be trials and sorrows, but He had "overcome the world" (John 16:33 NKJV). He is bigger than our obstacles, our pain, and our wilderness seasons. And with Him, we are more than conquerors!

I whined. I was impatient. I got frustrated, and I still do. But now when I do, I've changed my perceptions and instead focus on the truth of who God is. During trials, tribulations, and tough times, the most valuable lesson I learned was to refocus my thoughts and to trust God and to receive His love. I memorized this:

> Trust in the Lord with all your heart, and lean
> not on your own understanding; in all your ways
> acknowledge Him, and He shall direct your paths.
> (Proverbs 3:5–6 NKJV)

In this *now* moment of your life, let these words settle in your heart, soul and spirit. Trust is a decision in our head and an act of the will in our heart.

When Paul was in prison he learned the secret of being content was by focusing on God. When I learned more and more about the Trinity and their desire for my best interests, I actually began to say, "Thank you" in my trials. I came to realize that during the tough times I was being molded and shaped into a new and better version of myself. Who wants to remain their same old self? I don't.

Frequently I said to myself, "If Paul could be content in prison, surely I can be content in my comfortable condo!" When I trusted God and focused on Him instead of my problems, I felt peaceful. I saw Him in action. My faith grew. I saw Him come through time and time again. I prayed and my prayers were answered. Not all my prayers have been answered, but that doesn't prevent me from asking.

**Ask with faith.
Hope with expectation.
Believe with anticipation.**

How do we handle feeling pulled in different directions or worried? By being prayerful throughout the day and talking to God. We can tell Him every detail of every tough time in our life—past, current, and future. Then His peace, which is beyond our human understanding, makes the answers known to us through Jesus and through Holy Spirit.

Trials, hardships, and tough times are opportunities for our faith and hope to increase. In the darkness of the wilderness, I learned God's Word was always where I could turn for truth. I trusted that Jesus was there for me because He said, "I will never leave you nor forsake you" (Hebrews 13:5 NKJV).

Opportunities While Waiting

Just as the desert prepared Jesus for His future, our wilderness times prepare us when we are open to it. The conquering of our adversities prepares us for our future. As you work through challenges, keep your eyes on God and know you were created for an awesome and amazing purpose! Bill Johnson, pastor of Bethel Church in Redding, California, said "Every defeat you've ever had is only temporary. Every victory is permanent. It's just the way the kingdom works."

God gets us. He understands everything about us. And when we go through stressful trials, He is right there with us.

He can take our painful times and turn them into our powerful times of conquering.

I didn't know Jesus as healer until I had been hurt. He turned my pain into an opportunity rather than an obstacle. And while I didn't like or understand the pain, I eventually learned to acknowledge it and work through it because I honestly believed it was somehow preparing me for something better in the future. Jesus always knows and relates to how you feel. He already experienced every emotion imaginable while on earth. He turned over tables in the temple when He was angry. He sweat blood when He was afraid. He wept when a friend died. He was joyful when people were healed. And He loved to the point of dying on a cross so that you and I would have eternal life in heaven.

The love of God, Jesus, and Holy Spirit is always available to help you conquer the wilderness. It's profound and yet at the same time simple:

~ Receive Jesus as the Savior of the world who said, "I have overcome the world."

~ Ask forgiveness for wrongdoings.

~ Open your soul, spirit, and heart to the love of the Trinity.

Jesus said, "You will do greater things than I" and because we are made in His image we too can overcome and conquer all of our tough times.

Believing, receiving, and applying these truths ultimately will take you to a glorious, unimaginable, magnificent, never-ending eternity in heaven!

God's love and purpose meet us in the wilderness.

TOOLBOX

- We decide who we want to be friends with, who we want a relationship with. Why would you want a relationship with God, Jesus, and Holy Spirit? Are there any reasons you would not want to have a relationship with them?

- What tools have you learned to give you more patience and trust the next time you are waiting?

- During a wilderness season what opportunities came along that prepared you for the future?

- What do you think about God wanting you to know Him as Father? About Jesus wanting to be your friend? About Holy Spirit wanting to be your Comforter?

- The next time you're in the wilderness where will you turn? What will you do?

CHAPTER 10

MORE THAN CONQUERORS

"In all these things we are more than
conquerors through Him who loved us."
(Romans 8:37 NKJV)

Y ou've read the stories from my heart including intimate details of my life. Why did I share all this? The answer is simple and simultaneously profound. I've shared these deeply personal stories because like you, I've gone through drama, trauma, and chaotic wilderness seasons. I shared with you how I got through them and what I learned along the way. My heart's desire is for you to be able to get through your wilderness seasons with more understanding, more hope, and greater peace. Can we all say "yes" to more peace in our lives?

Eventually I got through those tumultuous times with intentional awareness of how I felt, what I thought, what I communicated to myself and others, what I chose to eat and drink, what I chose to listen to and not listen to, what I chose to read and to not read, and what I chose to do and not do. In addition to addressing my physical healing with holistic doctors and also prayer, one of the best decisions I made was to run after and embrace inner healing. Inner healing allowed me to work through negative emotions and painful experiences from the past thereby freeing and restoring my soul, spirit, and heart.

While writing the final pages of this book, I discovered my favorite place to write. I sit in a comfy chair, turned facing a window overlooking a ravine filled with high towering trees framed by a wall of lush, green plant life. To my right a door opens to my upper balcony offering a sweeping view of the forest. What now is a sanctuary of peace was once my most painful place.

When I was growing up Sunday was family day. Dad, mom and siblings, grandparents, aunts, uncles, and cousins, gathered for the entire afternoon featuring huge dinners with the best food on the planet! Or, more intimate time was spent with the immediate family. After the divorce my son spent most weekends with his father. Sunday afternoon rolled around, and I sat looking out that very window—alone. Tears poured down my face. My heart longed to be with someone, anyone, a family member or even a friend. Pain seared my heart. The divorce hurt, the loneliness hurt, and I wasn't equipped with the tools to handle those tough times.

But now that has changed. On any Sunday afternoon I can sit looking out the same window with joy and peace. Now, through implementing the tools described throughout this book, I can look out, knowing that God is with me, Jesus heals, and Holy Spirit is my Comforter.

Healing

You've read the stories: I lived with family dysfunction, was married and divorced, experienced the suicide of a husband, lost a child during a pregnancy, and had tons of health issues. I was broken. I recognized that I was broken, needed help, and I was ready to get it. And that is when God, in my weakness, gave me His strength. He knew what I needed!

I didn't want to live the rest of my life messed up and hurting, so I made a choice. I embraced a mental, emotional, and spiritual overhaul. In this process I attended healing rooms at churches, spent time with spiritual and professional counselors, and participated in prayer ministry training. I was like an onion; the old pain, traumas, and dysfunctions were peeled away one layer at a time. Was it uncomfortable? Sure. Bringing up old hurtful stuff can be painful, but only for a little while. As I worked through the wounds and began to heal, the person God created me to be emerged like a butterfly from a cocoon.

There was a key—one special key—to conquering the wilderness. With that key, the door opened into a place where the darkness lifted and I was healed, set free, and delivered from the past. That door opened to the light and presence of God's love.

"For You, O Lᴏʀᴅ, are my lamp;
the Lᴏʀᴅ illumines and dispels my
darkness." (2 Samuel 22:29 ᴀᴍᴘ)

Being Close to God

Here's how you can be close to God:
~ Read what the Bible says about Him and what He says
  in it.
~ Talk about Him with others.
~ Turn your heart (inner yearnings) to His promises.
~ Make Him the pleasure of your life.
~ Know and trust peace and fulfillment are in Him.
~ Give Him the right to direct your life (aka being
  obedient).
~ Commit your ways to Him and He will give you your
  desires in alignment with His will.

God is my rock and my light in the wilderness. In that
place, in His presence, is where I have total peace, safety, and
acceptance. A place where:
~ I can share anything and everything.
~ I can cry, yell, be mad or sad, and be understood.
~ I can be happy and joyful.
~ I am completely forgiven and where I daily learn to
  forgive others and myself.
~ I have no fear because I totally trust God, Jesus, and
  Holy Spirit.
~ I am unconditionally loved.

This is the place of God's love. I'll say it again, in my head I can't understand a love of such great magnitude, but in my heart I believe, receive, and accept it. Why did I write this book? Because I believe I have God's heart regarding the most important matter in life.

"The Lord is not slow in keeping his promise, as some understand slowness. Instead he is patient with you, not wanting *anyone* to perish, but *everyone* to come to repentance. (2 Peter 3:9 NIV, emphasis added)

God desires that "none should perish," which means spending forever in hell, which is described as a blazing furnace where the fire never goes out! When our physical bodies leave this planet, our spirit and resurrected bodies transition from this earthly existence to an eternal experience. Eternity is forever and ever and ever. The biggest decision you will ever make in life is whether or not you believe Jesus Christ is the Son of God. When you do believe it, your eternity is heaven where there are no more tears, no more pain, and no more sorrows. It is a paradise so glorious it can't be described with human words. I know where I'm spending eternity. Hope to see you there.

The ultimate Trusted Tool is . . .

TOGETHER WITH GOD, WE CAN CONQUER ANYTHING!

DECLARATIONS TO SAY TO YOURSELF EVERY DAY

1. I am a winner. (2 Cor. 2:14)

2. I am an adequate person. (2 Cor. 3:4-6)

3. I am unique and special. (1 Pet. 2:9)

4. My life has purpose. (Eph. 2:10)

5. I am successful. (Ps. 1:1-3)

6. I am strong and able. (Ps. 27:1)

7. I am sufficient for every task. (Phil. 4:13)

8. I overcome every obstacle. (John 16:33)

9. I am more than a conqueror. (Rom. 8:37)

10. I have divine protection. (Isa. 54:17)

11. I am secure and confident. (Prov. 3:24-26)

12. Under trial, I will stand. (1 Cor. 10:13)

13. My works shall prosper. (1 Kings 2:2-3)

14. I am well supplied. (Ps. 34:9-10)

15. Health and prosperity are mine. (3 John 2)

16. I live in abundance. (Phil. 4:19)

17. I am well and healthy. (Matt. 8:16-17)

18. My thoughts are positive. (Phil. 4:6-9)

19. I am filled with God's peace. (Phil. 4:7)

20. My faith is strongly working. (Heb. 4:14)

21. I am a totally new person. (2 Cor. 5:17)

22. I am happy, happy, happy! (Phil. 4:4)

23. I am free! I am free! (John 8:32)

24. All this is true, and I believe it! (Num. 23:19-20)

25. I envision each affirmation. (1 Chron. 29:18)

HEALING RESOURCES

Dr. Douglas Carr, Freedom Ministries,
https://www.dcfreedomministry.com

American Association of Christian Counselors,
https://www.aacc.net

Psychology Today, https://www.psychologytoday.com/us/
therapists

Suicide and Crisis Hotline: Dial 988 or 911, Text 838255

New Life Ministries, https://newlife.com

Women of Faith, 100+ Biblically based resources,
https://www.womenoffaith.com/resources

Brain Life Center, https://brainlifecenter.com,
248-922-9490

NOTES

1   Rebecca Lake, "Listening Statistics: 23 Facts You Need to Hear," Credit Donkey, September 17, 2015, https://www.creditdonkey.com/listening-statistics.html.

2   "Anger: An Urgent Plea for Justice and Action," https://emotionalcompetency.com/anger.htm.

3   Sarah Berry, "Fragranced products are making us sick, study finds," *Sunday Morning Herald*, March 6, 2017.

4   Brandi Koskie and Crystal Raypole, "Depression Facts and Statistics," Healthline, January 14, 2022, https://www.healthline.com/health/depression/facts-statistics-infographic#1.

5   Does God love everyone? Yes, He shows mercy and kindness to all. Does God love Christians more than He loves non-Christians? No, not in regard to His merciful love. Does God love Christians in a different way than He loves non-Christians? Yes, because believers have exercised faith in God's Son, they are saved. God has a unique relationship with Christians in that only Christians have forgiveness based on God's eternal grace. The unconditional, merciful love God has for everyone should bring us to faith, receiving with gratefulness the conditional, covenant love He grants those who receive Jesus Christ as Savior. (Got Questions, https://www.gotquestions.org/does-God-love-everyone.html.)

6   https://theblazingcenter.com/2019/02/trusting-god.html

ABOUT THE AUTHOR

Lana Kristal is a speaker, author, and encourager. From the time she was a teenager, and to the present day Lana's friends turn to her for advice and counsel—and she loves it! Lana now shares knowledge and wisdom in her first book, *Conquering the Wilderness: Trusted Tools for Tough Times*.

Her personal journey through illness, the loss of a child, divorce, and suicide of a husband presented opportunities to conquer life's challenges. Lana's heart is to share with others how to overcome difficulties and live the best life possible.

Lana's life is full of variety. She is a mother and ministry leader, and has been a waitress, model, and dental hygienist as well as an entrepreneur and philanthropist. She was a suicide prevention keynote speaker, a "She Leads Michigan" honoree, a guest at the White House on National Gold Star Wives Day, and co-leader of the Michigan National Day of Prayer.

Lana loves people and family, loves to help others, and loves to speak the truth. Encourage one another and build one another up is Lana's life mission.

Printed in the USA
CPSIA information can be obtained
at www.ICGtesting.com
JSHW020512171123
52253JS00005B/16